From Cameroonian to American Citizen

A Journey of Faith

Eric Tangumonkem, Ph.D.

PO Box 831001, Richardson, TX 75080
A Subsidiary of IEM APPROACH

©2020 by Eric Tangumonkem. All rights reserved.

IEM PRESS (PO Box 831001, Richardson, TX 75080) functions only as a book publisher. As such, the ultimate design, content, editorial accuracy, and views expressed or implied in this work are those of the author. No part of this publication may be reproduced, stored in a retrieval system, or transmitted in any way by any means—electronic, mechanical, photocopy, recording, or otherwise—without the prior permission of the copyright holder, except as provided by USA copyright law. Unless otherwise noted, all Scriptures are taken from the Holy Bible, New International Version®, NIV®. Copyright © 1973 1978, 1984, 2011 by Biblica, Inc.™ Used by permission of Zondervan. All rights reserved worldwide. www. zondervan.com ISBN

ISBN 13: 978-1-63603-002-9
Library of Congress Catalog Card Number: 2020943662

To my wife, Elizabeth Tayem,
for standing by me through thick and thin and encouraging
me to do what is right

Table of Contents

Foreword Vii

Preface ix

Chapter One: The First F-1 Visa 1

Chapter Two: The First F-2 Visa 19

Chapter Three: The Second F-1 Visa.............................. 23

Chapter Four: H-1B Visa and H-4 Visa 25

Chapter Five: The B-2 Visa 29

Chapter Six: The Second F-1 Visa.............................. 33

Chapter Seven: DV Lottery 39

Chapter Eight: US Citizenship 47

Chapter Nine: The Discussion that We as a
Country Need to Have 55

Chapter Ten: The Way Forward 65

Chapter Eleven: An Eternal perspective 83

Acknowledgments.. 95

About Missional University 97

Foreword

I am honored to write this foreword for my former student, Eric Tangumonkem, whom I have mentored and watched mature for fifteen years. This is not a book based in academic theory; rather, it is one man's personal account of how—and why—he successfully navigated the complexities and challenges of a broken United States immigration system.

I met Eric in 2002, a few days after he arrived in the United States to pursue a doctoral degree in geosciences at The University of Texas at Dallas. As an international student from Cameroon with no scholarships and little cash, Eric was confronted directly and immediately with the challenges of being an international student in a foreign country. He had three choices: quit and go back home, break the law, or move forward. From day one, Eric made a conscious decision to stay in school no matter what.

Instead of complaining about the unfairness of the system, his financial pressures, and emotional difficulties (separation from his wife and young son), he faced every challenge head on. He made a commitment to become part of the solution—to add value to other people and to ensure that the blessings he received in America were passed on to others.

With time and through Divine Providence he overcame all, reunited with his wife and son, won the Green Card lottery, and in 2016 became a proud citizen of the United States of America. Eric demonstrated that it is possible to immigrate legally and to realize the American Dream—to become all that you desire to be by working hard and doing what is right, even when circumstances make it very difficult.

Why I Refused to Become an Illegal Alien by Eric Tangumonkem is a compelling story that will not disappoint. On the pages that follow, the author offers a cautionary warning to the country to take a deeper and closer look at the issues at hand and to provide real solutions now—to do more than simply relieve the [often self-imposed] suffering of immigrants by taking a stand for truth and justice.

Happy reading and deep reflections,
Dr. James Carter
Geosciences Professor Emeritus
The University of Texas at Dallas

Preface

Fifteen years ago I landed at the Dallas-Fort Worth International Airport with a single suitcase. I showed up believing that by the grace of God everything would work out as it should. Little did I know that it would take fourteen years of sleepless nights and thousands of dollars to remain in the US legally—fourteen years to become a citizen of the United States of America.

At one point I had no money, no job, and no work permit, and my wife and four kids were depending on me to provide for them. I was tempted to violate my visa status and become an illegal immigrant—an undocumented alien—by letting my visa lapse, but I chose the only legal option that was available to me at the time—to go back to school so I could be placed on a student visa. I already had a PhD in geosciences, but I went back to school and enrolled in an MBA program. Paying for this degree would mean incurring thousands of dollars of debt without knowing how it would be paid, but I understood that as a believer in Jesus Christ, I was to walk by faith (2 Corinthians 5:7–10).

I approach the issue of illegal immigration with humility and trepidation because it is an extremely sensitive one. That being said, there is a strong need for us as a country to talk about this elephant in the room.

According to some estimates, there are close to fifteen million illegal immigrants in the United States of America. These people are living in the shadows, and each day they are afraid of being deported. Some of them have children who were born here, and they are raising these children under extremely difficult circumstances. These illegal immigrants are literally under "country arrest" because if they leave the United States, they might never be able to come back in.

The purpose of this book is to highlight the struggles and the price being paid by those who come to the United States having made a conscious decision to obey the law—those who make the deliberate, costly, and difficult choice to be legal immigrants instead of staying in the country illegally or undocumented. What makes obeying US immigration laws so important to these individuals? What inspires and motivates them to do what is right? Unfortunately, little or nothing is being said about this class of people as the country debates and grapples with the challenges of illegal immigration and undocumented aliens. Mostly you hear about the plight of those who are here illegally and how to ease their misery. But what about those who are here legally? What about those outside of the country who are trying to come in through the right channels? Everyone accepts that the system is broken, but the solutions to fix it are dividing the country.

The book you are reading is my personal story of why I refused to become an illegal alien and the huge price I paid to remain in the US legally over a fourteen-year period. It is a chronological account of my journey through the American immigration system, highlighting the good, the bad, and the ugly of standing up for and doing what is right. I do not write on behalf of all immigrants; this is my personal experience told to the best of my ability. I hope it will shed light on a very pertinent and challenging issue that needs serious attention. We cannot afford to keep kicking the can to the next generation; we will pay a huge price in the future if this issue is not resolved.

CHAPTER ONE

The First F-1 Visa: Baptism by Fire

Sixteen years ago I attended a conference organized by the Geological Society of Africa in Yaounde, the capital of Cameroon, to present a paper showcasing some findings of my geological field research. One afternoon, I had an "aha" moment: I felt the Holy Spirit nudging me to travel to the United States for graduate studies.

This was not going to be an easy task based on the circumstances surrounding me at that time. My wife and I were a few months into our marriage and expecting our first child, and I was still a student without a stable job. I was supporting the two of us by tutoring other students. Going to the United States was the furthest thing from my mind. The US is quite far from Cameroon, and the cost of education for international students is extremely expensive. In addition, I had to pass a test of English as a foreign language (TOEFL) and the Graduate Record Exam (GRE). Raising the money to take these exams was one thing and passing them—especially the GRE—was another matter altogether.

When I went home, I told my wife that God was asking us to go to the United States of America and that we were going to pray our way to the US. She agreed to pray with me, and we began making preparations.[1]

After a year of communicating back and forth with The University of Texas at Dallas, I received word that I had been admitted into the graduate program in the geosciences department. I was hoping the university would grant me admission with financial assistance, but no scholarship or teaching assistantship was offered.

My admission letter instructed me to send documentation demonstrating that I would be able to pay for my education in the US, including tuition, fees, supplies, room, board, transportation, and medical expenses. The cost in my currency was about eleven million CFA francs, which was an enormous amount of money for us. We were between a rock and a hard place. We did all we could to raise the money, including asking my church for help, but to no avail. Not surprisingly, God intervened and raised up a Moses to part the Atlantic Ocean for us! A friend took out a loan in her name for the sole purpose of supporting us as we stepped out in obedience to God's call. She loaned us the money, and one of my uncles helped with the required financial documents. We had always been firm believers in avoiding debt and living within our means, but higher education seemed like a smart investment, and a

---

[1] Eric Tangumonkem, *Coming to America: A Journey of Faith* (Richardson: IEM Press, 2014).

favorable exchange rate meant that paying off such a large debt would be much easier once I got to the US.

One year after I received the call to come to America, I was ready to get my visa. School would be starting in a couple of months, and I wanted to arrive early to work a little and earn some money before then.

When I got to the embassy, the Consular Officer who interviewed me refused to issue the visa. He said I should transfer the money I had in a local Cameroonian bank into one of the more renowned international banks. To say that I was disappointed would be an understatement. This first visa denial devastated me and almost killed my dream of coming to the US. I had to go back to the friend who was helping me with the money to plead with her to move the money to a different bank. After the money was moved, my F-1 visa[2] was issued with less than one week until the start of classes. The very next day, I would be on a plane to the US with one suitcase and three million CFA francs,[3] which I had borrowed at an interest rate of ten percent.

A lot of people came to the airport to see me off—my wife and infant son, my parents and in-laws, my brothers and sisters, aunts and uncles, cousins, nieces, and friends. Everyone was excited for me to be traveling to the land where everything was possible—the land of great opportunity and abundance. Based on the stories I had heard about the US, there were tons of jobs, and all I

---

[2] The F-1 visa is a non-immigrant student visa that allows foreigners to pursue education in the United States

[3] Three million CFA francs is equivalent to three thousand US dollars.

had to do was show up, secure a job, make some money, and start to pay back the debt as soon as possible. I found myself imagining all the great things I would acquire in the United States of America. First, I would get my wife and son to join me, and then I would help with the education of my younger brothers, and then my extended family.

Everyone insisted that I not forget to call when I get there and made me promise to keep in touch. As a child, we had heard stories of family members who had traveled abroad—especially to the United States—and had lost all communication with their parents. Some had been living abroad for more than thirty years with absolutely no communication with their families. The more fortunate families would hear from their loved ones occasionally but were left to wonder why they could not come back home to visit. I came to understand that some of these people did not have papers. What did "not having papers" mean? Then I heard that one needed a Green Card to be able to travel in and out of the country. What was "a Green Card?" How do you get one? Was it not a matter of simply applying to get one?

There were many questions going through my mind as I boarded the plane that night. I hugged my wife and with a heavy heart slowly eased out of her embrace. As she cried, I felt the full weight of the journey I was about to embark upon. I promised her that within a year she and our son would join me.

One of my greatest fears was that I would be refused entry into the US. We had heard stories of people who had acquired visas but were refused when they arrived at the port of entry. The events of 9/11 added more anxiety because of some of the changes the US Department of Homeland Security had made.

My flight landed at Newark International Airport in New Jersey, and I was successfully processed and granted entry. I took my last flight to Dallas, and when I arrived, Dr. Duane Collins, a former missionary to Cameroon who had met my parents in the 1970s, met me at the airport. The next day, he and I drove to The University of Texas at Dallas (UTD) and were directed to the international student office, where I received instructions on what to do next. I was on my own from that point forward.

My first need was for a place to sleep since I had not applied for student housing. I was told that a room would open in a four-bedroom apartment for me the next day, so I applied for the room and completed the necessary paperwork. Then the president of the African Student Association (ASA) took me to his house off campus where I spent the night. The following morning, I went to student housing to sign my lease and was shocked at the cost of the room. My rent would be two hundred AND twenty- six dollars plus utilities! How was I going to pay for this? I had a little over two thousand dollars on me, and my tuition was two thousand dollars and a few hundred. I had no choice but to sign the lease and get into the apartment. There was no bed or furniture in the apartment, so I slept on the floor for the first couple of nights. This was not the America I was expecting, to say the least.

The next day I went to new student orientation, and what I heard was *more than* shocking. The international student office explained to us what an F-1 visa is— including all of its restrictions—and stressed the importance of staying in status. First, a student with an F-1 visa had to be enrolled in school at all times and taking the required number of credit hours. (Undergraduate students needed to take at least twelve credit hours per semester; graduate students, nine.) Second, an F-1 student could work only on campus, and the maximum number of hours allowed by law each week was twenty. International student tuition was about fifty percent higher than what American students paid, and yet on-campus jobs paid only the minimum wage. Working off campus was allowed only under dire circumstances, such as when a primary sponsor stops support because of crisis or death. And even if an F-1 student's sponsor dies, the student must wait a full year before applying for economic hardship. Approval of economic hardship can be a lengthy process, during which time the F1 student must maintain full-time status. How is that even possible?! The international student office reiterated that F-1 students caught working off campus would be in violation of their visa status and as such, would be in the country illegally. Also, F-1 students who failed to renew their passport, allowing it to expire, would be violating their visa status and risk being kicked out of school and the country. I left the orientation with a clear understanding that I was expected by law to be in status throughout my stay in the US. I made up my mind, right then and there, to obey the law no matter what because it was the right and godly thing to do. The following verse guided my decision:

> *If you do what is right, you won't need to be afraid of your rulers. But watch out if you do what is wrong! You don't want to be afraid of those in authority, do you? Then do what is right, and you will be praised. The one in authority serves God for your good. But if you do wrong, watch out! Rulers don't carry a sword for no reason at all. They serve God. And God is carrying out his anger through them. The ruler punishes anyone who does wrong. You must obey the authorities. Then you will not be punished. You must also obey them because you know it is right. (Romans 13:3–5)*

The issue here is not the fairness or unfairness of the laws and restrictions placed on international students; rather it is that obedience to God requires keeping the law. I believe my first responsibility is to honor God in all that I do. It was not possible to disobey the US immigration laws without violating my conscience and breaking God's laws as well.

The following passage of scripture written by the apostle Peter emphasizes the necessity of obeying those in authority and highlights the negative consequences that may befall those who walk in disobedience:

> *Follow the lead of every human authority. Do this for the Lord's sake. Obey the emperor. He is the highest authority. Obey the governors. The emperor sends them to punish those who do wrong. He also sends them to praise those who do right. By doing good, you will put a stop to the talk of foolish people. They don't know what they are saying. Live as free people. But don't use your freedom to cover up evil. Live as people who are God's slaves. (1 Peter 2:13–16)*

There is punishment for those who break the law, and in my case as an international student on an F-1 visa, violating status could have resulted in my being deported. When a student gets out of status, it is difficult for him to be reinstated. He will live in the country without the possibility of legal employment and fair wages. This is when other unscrupulous people—lawbreakers as well— will hire him and take advantage of him.

After orientation, I went to the geosciences department to inquire about becoming a teaching assistant. The department chair told me that all the teaching assistant positions had been filled and there was nothing he could do for me. His repose was perplexing. I explained to him that I did not have enough money to pay for tuition, books, room, and board, and he in turn explained to me that "there are many jobs in the area, and most of our students work and go to school, so go get a job."

Go get a job?! Where and how?! During orientation I had been categorically told that working off campus was illegal and could lead to my losing F-1 visa status and eventually being deported. If this happened, the whole purpose of my leaving my home country and flying more than eight thousand miles to Dallas would be defeated. I kept wondering if he did not know what the law said concerning F-1 students and employment. I told him that it was not possible for me to work off campus.

When I left his office, I went and registered for the nine graduate credit hours that the law required. The cost was more than four thousand dollars; I had a little over two thousand dollars on me. How was I going to pay for these classes? I had signed up for them, but to be officially registered, I had to pay for them. Not paying before the deadline could jeopardize my legal status in the country, and I certainly did not want this to happen. I went to the bursar's office and described my predicament. The person I spoke with made it clear that there was little the school could do to help. The only solution would be for me to take out a student loan, which I did, to cover the remaining balance.

I was extremely uncomfortable taking out a loan because I did not know how I would pay it back.

Remember, the two thousand dollars I had on me had been borrowed in Cameroon at ten percent a month. Getting deeper into debt was the last thing I wanted, but there was no other option for me at that time. I now had no money, but at least I was happy to be registered for my classes and to know that I was in the country legally.

All this had transpired within the course of a week. I called it a baptism of fire. All the talk of tons of jobs in America—working and going to school—did not add up. American students could work and go to school, but international students on F-1 visas had almost zero chance. It became clear that I would not be able to send money back to Cameroon to support my wife and son as we had anticipated. This also meant that I could not start paying back the loan I had borrowed to pay my airfare and part of my tuition.

I was homesick and broke, and the immigration law was making an already difficult and stressful situation dire. The temptation to do something about my situation became extremely strong. Some people I spoke with warned me that if I did not do something quickly to change my status, my stay in the US would be difficult and miserable. They advised me to do all I could to get a Green Card[4], which would enable me to work and go to school. They were right in saying that without legal papers my life in the country would be miserable, but they were wrong in suggesting that I get involved in illegal and questionable activities in order to solve my dilemma.

One option they presented to me was to get married to a US citizen, who would petition for me to get a Green Card. Of course, I could not make use of this option because I was already married. I had a wife and son in Cameroon. When I explained this to those giving me advice, they laughed at me and explained that I could fake a marriage.

---

[4] The Green Card is a permit allowing a foreign national to live and work permanently in the US.

To do this meant paying money to any woman who would agree to marry me. We would go to court and get married, and then divorce and part ways after my Green Card is issued. To me, this was playing with fire. My reasons for rejecting this option were many:

1. My marriage vows would have been compromised significantly. *"Therefore what God has joined together, let no one separate" (Mark 10:9).* This included trying to get a Green Card in the United States.
2. I would have been living a lie.
3. The woman I would have paid to marry me might change her mind and want it to be a real marriage.
4. There was the potential for me to commit adultery and destroy my marriage.

One day as I was riding the city bus back to campus, I engaged in conversation with the driver. It turns out that he was originally from West Africa and had solved his paper situation by concocting a fake marriage. He claimed that it was his only option and that it was Divine Providence that had made the scheme possible. *How could he say such a thing?!* I told him that his course of action was wrong! To defend himself, he revealed to me that he had been raised in the church and his parents were elders. I wondered in my heart if we had been reading the same Bible and practicing the same faith.

The fake marriage idea just did not make sense to me, despite the fact that I was told by many people to do it. Well, I am not "many people;" I am me, a child of God, and I believe the right thing has to be done even when circumstances make it hard to do. The fact that "many people" are doing something does not make it right! Living with integrity does not come easily; there is always a price to be paid. I was willing to pay that price, so I said no to divorcing my wife and faking a marriage for the sake of changing my non-immigrant status to immigrant status. Another option was for me to declare political asylum. This suggestion was the most frequent one I heard from those trying to help me. One person said, "I know of pastors who have declared political asylum *(implying that if pastors would do it, surely it was okay for me to do it)*. Life is going to be so difficult for you to the point that you will be willing

> *Now there was a famine in the land, and Abram went down to Egypt to live there for a while because the famine was severe. As he was about to enter Egypt, he said to his wife Sarai, "I know what a beautiful woman you are. When the Egyptians see you, they will say, 'This is his wife.' Then they will kill me but will let you live. Say you are my sister so that I will be treated well for your sake and my life will be spared because of you." When Abram came to Egypt, the Egyptians saw that Sarai was a very beautiful woman. And when Pharaoh's officials saw her, they praised her to Pharaoh, and she was taken into his palace. He treated Abram well for her sake, and Abram acquired sheep and cattle, male and female donkeys, male and female servants, and camels. (Genesis 12:10–16)*

Based on his interpretation, Abraham lied to avoid being killed by Pharaoh, and God forgave him. In my situation, he reasoned, God would forgive me if I lie and then confess. He rationalized that to do this would be better than to fall into the hands of "Pharaoh" (The United States of America). According to this individual, Abraham lied and instead of being punished gained more stuff; therefore, it is okay for us to lie to get what we want. I found this interpretation presumptuous and lacking in substance. The Bible does not sanction what Abraham did! I would rather allow this scripture to direct my conduct:

> *Do not be deceived: God cannot be mocked. A man reaps what he sows. Whoever sows to please their flesh, from the flesh will reap destruction; whoever sows to please the Spirit, from the Spirit will reap eternal life. Let us not become weary in doing good, for at the proper time we will reap a harvest if we do not give up. (Galatians 6:7–8)*

The law of reaping and sowing is universal; it is not a respecter of persons. Organizing a fake marriage or lying that I was running away from political persecution for the purpose of getting papers is sowing in the flesh, and I would not do it.

The pressure to do something about my situation was mounting, but I resolved that I would not yield to temptation. During this time, I drew a lot of inspiration from Joseph, who is one of my favorite Bible heroes. Joseph refused to commit adultery with his master's wife even though he was a slave and was completely at the mercy of his mistress. The events unfolded as follows:

> *Now Joseph was well-built and handsome, and after a while, his master's wife took notice of Joseph and said, "Come to bed with me!" But he refused. "With me in charge," he told her, "my master does not concern himself with anything in the house; everything he owns he has entrusted to my care. No one is greater in this house than I am. My master has withheld nothing from me except you because you are his wife. How then could I do such a wicked thing and sin against God?" And though she spoke to Joseph day after day, he refused to go to bed with her or even be with her. One day he went into the house to attend to his duties, and none of the household servants was inside. She caught him by his cloak and said, "Come to bed with me!" But he left his cloak in her hand and ran out of the house. (Genesis 39:8–12)*

It is amazing that Joseph chose to do the right thing instead of complaining. He could have tried justifying his sin by blaming it on his mistress. After all, she was the one who brought up the idea and persistently pursued him. Who knows, but he might have gained his freedom by meeting his mistress' needs. She might have talked with his master to release him. If you look at this situation superficially, you might say Joseph took an unnecessary risk by not obeying his master's wife, but Joseph was not gambling. Undoubtedly, he had heard how his great-grandfather, Abraham, had obeyed God when asked to take his son with him to Mount Moriah. Abraham tied him up, laid him on the altar, pulled out his knife, lifted it up, and was about to strike when God told him not to. Instead, God provided a lamb for Abraham to sacrifice.

The principle here is that of gain through loss, or life by way of death. We know this principle is important because Jesus Christ talked about it during his earthly ministry:

> *Whoever tries to keep their life will lose it, and whoever loses their life will preserve it. (Luke 17:33)*
>
> *Jesus replied, "The hour has come for the Son of Man to be glorified. Very truly I tell you, unless a kernel of wheat falls to the ground and dies, it remains only a single seed. But if it dies, it produces many seeds. Anyone who loves their life will lose it, while anyone who hates their life in this world will keep it for eternal life. Whoever serves me must follow me; and where I am, my servant also will be. My Father will honor the one who serves me. (John 12:20–33)*

I persevered in spite of all the pressure I was under because I believed that standing for what is right requires paying a price. Here I was without money, without papers to work, and unable to send money back to Cameroon to support my wife and young son, but I chose not to lie or engage in unethical behavior in order to alleviate my pain. I was being called to lay America on the altar and sacrifice it. I was so thrilled to be here in the United States that I would have done almost anything to remain here, but like Abraham and Joseph, I gave up what I held dear in order that I might keep it.

By the end of the first semester, I ran completely out of money. Without divine intervention there would be no way for me to stay in school. There was nothing I could do to change my situation. I did not have an on-campus job, and even if I did, the pay would not have been enough to cover my education and related expenses. To make more money, I had to secure a good-paying job, and to secure a good-paying job, I had to obtain work authorization. Some suggested that I buy a fake social security number or use someone else's social security number that had no restrictions on it, and then I would simply share my pay with the person whose social security number I had used. People who let others use their social security number to work say they are "helping," but how can you enable falsehood and lack of character development and call it help? There was no way I was going to go down this slippery slope! It was incumbent on me to do what was morally right no matter how difficult it was.

I believed that ungodly counsel should never be followed no matter how enticing it may appear. My focus was not on immediate relief but on the long-term impact of my present decisions. These words from Psalms comforted me:

> *Blessed is the man who does not walk in the counsel of the wicked or stand in the way of sinners or sit in the seat of mockers. But his delight is in the law of the LORD, and on his law he meditates day and night. He is like a tree planted by streams of water, which yields its fruit in season and whose leaf does not wither. Whatever he does prospers. (Psalm 1:1–3)*

My desire was to prosper in the United States of America. I understood that that would come at a price, and I had made up my mind that I would pay that price no matter what. This was not a popular, comfortable, or desirable stand, but it was the noble, honorable, and right thing to do.

One week before the beginning of the spring semester, I received word that the geosciences department at the university had made me a teaching assistant. This meant I would not have to worry about tuition, fees, room, and board. Thank God, I could stay in school, but my challenges were far from over. I was still highly indebted. The interest rate on the loan I had taken out before traveling to the United States was ten percent monthly, and it was compounding fast. My stipend of eleven hundred dollars a month was not enough for me to pay off the loan as quickly as I had hoped. My wife and son were still in Cameroon, and I longed to bring them over to be with me. All I could do was to pray and wait.

CHAPTER TWO

The First F-2 Visa: What God Has Joined Together, Let Not Immigration Separate

The F-1 visa clearly states that it is a non-immigrant visa, but I had to come to the United States of America to fully understand what that meant. As an international student on a non-immigrant F-1 visa, I could not just get up one day and decide that I was going to stop going to school and instead go and get a job. I was here to go to school, and if I didn't go to school full time, I would be violating the terms of the visa and would risk deportation. Also, I could not just go and buy an airline ticket for my wife and son to join me; they too would need visas. But before visas would be issued, I would have to provide evidence that I had the means to support them here.

Most people around me suggested that I wait until I graduate and get a job to begin the process of bringing my family over to join me, but I believe families are meant to live and grow and learn together, and there was no point in keeping my wife and son in Cameroon. So I sent in the necessary documentation indicating that I would be able to support myself, my wife, and our son here in the US. (The cost was estimated at about twenty- four thousand dollars a year.) When my wife and son went to the United States Consulate in Yaounde with all these documents and applied for F-2 visas[5], their visas were denied! The reason the Consular Officer gave was that my wife did not have sufficient ties to Cameroon. I was shocked and confused. What was I to do? Our desire was to be together and not allow our economic situation to separate us. How could I prove to the United States Consulate in Cameroon that I had no intention of remaining in the United States after I graduate?

We did what we knew how to do—pray. And what God was leading us to do was one of the hardest things we could imagine. Similar to when Abraham's faith in God was put to the test regarding his willingness to sacrifice his son Isaac, our faith in God was also tested. Were we willing to surrender to God's will even if it meant leaving our son behind? The decision was made to leave our son in Cameroon in order to satisfy the Consulate's requirement that we demonstrate "strong ties" to our homeland. The overwhelming pain and anguish were nearly unbearable. A thousand and one thoughts ran through my mind of all the possible things that could go wrong. Most of all, I feared that my son would resent me for abandoning him in Cameroon so I could pursue a world-class education in

---

[5] The F-2 visa is a non-immigrant visa for spouses and dependents of F-1 students studying in the United States.

America. We had reliable, loving, and very capable family members who could take care of our son, but a part of me knew that nobody could love him and raise him like I would. The whole idea of leaving him behind made me sick, but there was nothing I could do. For my wife to go back to the embassy to ask to be considered again for an F-2 visa, she had to make some changes. Leaving our son behind felt like compelling enough proof that after school we would be coming back to Cameroon.

As my wife was flipping through her wallet to find her passport, the Consular Officer interviewing her—this time a different officer whom I believe was there by God's choosing—saw a picture of our son and asked where he was and why he was not travelling with her. My wife explained that she had been denied a visa the first time for lack of ties to the country, so this second time we had decided to keep him in the country to serve as our "strong ties." The Consular Officer asked my wife if she would like to travel with our son, and my wife's response was yes, of course. And even though my wife had not applied for our son, and he was not even at the embassy with her, the Consular Officer issued two F-2 visas on the spot—one for my wife and one for our son. At last they would be joining me in the United States. We had lived apart for one year.

CHAPTER THREE

The Second F-1 Visa: Raising a Family While Studying

After one year of being in the country, and while I was still in graduate school, my wife became pregnant and gave birth to a baby girl. Our daughter was born a United States citizen, with all of its rights and privileges. The difference between her restrictions and ours was like night and day. Her social security card was issued with only one restriction—that she not be allowed to work except by authorization of the Department of Homeland Security. We were happy knowing she would never have to deal with all the immigration challenges the rest of us were dealing with.

As we began to investigate the possibility of my wife going to school in the evenings after I got home and could watch the children, we discovered that she could neither enroll in any degree program on the F-2 visa nor get a job; the only option she had was to change her visa from F-2 to F-1. We borrowed money from friends and put it in a bank to show that we would be able to pay her tuition at the community college. An I-20[6] was issued, and she enrolled at Collin College. Now both us were on F-1 visas. She was required to take twelve credit hours each semester, and I had to take nine in order to comply with immigration laws.

Two years later, we had another daughter while both of us were students. The pressure to do something on the side to increase our income became extremely strong again, but we had little wiggle room in what the law permitted us to do. There was nothing we could do legally to change our status, and the only options available to us were, as previously noted, not really options at all. We were going to school, living on an extremely tight budget and under challenging living conditions, but we were determined to stay on the narrow path, keep the faith, pray, and hope for God's best.

---

6 The Form I-20, or Certificate of Eligibility for Nonimmigrant (F-1) Student Status, is a document issued by colleges, universities, and vocational schools that provides supporting information on a student's F or M status.

CHAPTER FOUR

H-1B Visa and H-4 Visa: Uncertainty, Perplexity, and a Costly Proposition

For almost six years I was on an F-1 visa, and during that time I could not legally get a job off campus to support my family. The heat was on, and I was getting worried. My family was in a constant state of uncertainty regarding our future because of restrictions associated with the F-1 visa. I could not apply, as American students did, for most of the scholarships that were available. I traveled great distances to attend oil and gas industry-sponsored events designed specifically to recruit summer interns but got nothing. I remember some of the American students receiving five or six internship offers from different companies, but few companies granted internships to international students. Some employers clearly stated on the application that students who rely on sponsorship would not be considered at all. As my graduation date drew nearer, uncertainty became stronger. I kept wondering how I was going to get a job after I graduated.

My fears and worries disappeared when a few months before graduation I went to a student job fair organized by the American Association of Petroleum Geologists (AAPG) and got a job offer from Schlumberger, one of the few companies that hired F-1 students and acquired H-1B visas[7] for them. By the grace of God, I was issued one. This meant that I could not work for a different employer even if I wanted to. The only way I could work for a different company was if the company transferred my H-1B. This gets tricky in a sluggish economy because of the high cost involved in all the paperwork. Also, companies must justify why they are hiring a foreign national rather than an American. For these reasons, many companies opt out of the program. This makes it difficult for international students to get jobs when they graduate, especially in difficult economic times.

Moving from an F-1 to an H-1B visa meant that my wife had to change her F-1 to an H-4 visa.[8] Fortunately for us, my wife graduated a few days before I did and was no longer in need of a student visa. It was our hope that Schlumberger would eventually change my H-B1 visa to a

---

[7] The H-1B visa is a temporary non-immigrant visa issued to foreign nationals who want to work in the US in specialty occupations.

[8] The H-4 visa is issued to the spouse and children of an H-1B holder who are less than 21 years old, allowing these dependents to enter and stay in the US legally.

Green Card, and then my wife would automatically become a permanent resident as well.

Finally, we were experiencing a much-needed break from the pressures and restrictions of being students on F-1 visas. My wife decided to take some time off and concentrate fully on the family. Little did we know that our lives were about to take a dramatic turn—one that would test our faith, our beliefs, and convictions.

CHAPTER FIVE

The B-2 Visa: Your Parents Are Not Allowed to Attend Your Graduation

I was defending my doctoral thesis at the same time as my wife was finishing her associate degree. With God's help, we had accomplished the unthinkable—two F-1 students raising three kids on a meager student stipend, and both of us graduating with degrees debt free.[9] I was the first person in my family to graduate with a doctorate, and my wife was also the first in her family to graduate with a college degree. This truly was a miracle, and it

---

[9] God's grace and provision had allowed us to repay our original high-interest loan in Cameroon within seven months. God further blessed me with a good-paying job with Schlumberger that allowed us to pay back all the money we had charged against our credit card to pay for my MBA.

called for celebration in a big way. Our graduation dates were scheduled for the same week. Her commencement ceremony would be on a Friday and mine on Saturday.

I went to the international student office as was required and informed them that I wanted my father, mother, and a close family friend to come over for my graduation. By this time, we had been in the country for almost six years without seeing our parents. Having them here for graduation was going to be especially meaningful to me since my father, who was an educator, had been my teacher in first, third, fifth, and sixth grades and had believed strongly in education at a high personal cost to him.[10] An invitation letter was issued for each of them. We mailed the letters to Cameroon and awaited the good news that they would be coming for my graduation. But the news was not what we expected.

My parents had been drilled on questions they might be asked during the interview, such as how long I had been in the United States, the name of the university I was graduating from, and the city I lived in. Unfortunately, the Consular Officer refused to grant them the B-2[11] visas. We were in shock and disbelief! What in the world was happening? Why would they deny my parents' attending my graduation?

---

[10] Eric Tangumonkem, *Seven Success Lessons Learned from My Father* (Richardson: IEM Press, 2016).

[11] The B-2 visa allows a foreigner to travel in the United States for pleasure, tourism, visiting with friends and family, or simply rest and recuperation.

Part of the reason, I learned, was that my parents might come to America and not return. I understood that rationale since I personally knew people whose parents and relatives had come to visit but stayed in the country and became illegal aliens. To curb this problem, the embassy decided to refuse to issue visas to my parents. This unilateral decision penalized us and threatened to rob me of the joy of sharing one of my greatest achievements with my greatest heroes.

We refused to take no for an answer. I went back to the international student office and asked for different invitation letters to be issued. This was done, and the letters were mailed to Cameroon. My parents went to the embassy a second time, applied for visas to travel, and were again denied.

The big day was drawing closer, and we were running out of options. In a last desperate attempt, we asked my father to go alone to try to get a visa; he was denied a third time. I was devastated, but there was nothing within my power that I could do. My father missed my graduation.

There is no logical explanation for what happened. After my graduation, I tried again to bring my father for a visit, and still he was turned down. In total, he appealed to the United States Consulate five times and was denied all five times. Is there a formula to explain why some people are issued visas and some are denied? I do not know. All I know is that it does not make sense. The system is broken and needs to be fixed.

CHAPTER SIX

The Second F-1 Visa: Back to Basics

When my wife and I graduated in May 2008, the United States was going through what was described by some as the worst economic crisis since The Great Depression. Many banks, companies, and other financial institutions were going under, and the economic outlook was bleak.

President George W. Bush was towards the end of his term, and the country seemed eager to see him out and usher in a new president. Barack Obama was the frontrunner for the Democratic Party and stood a good chance of becoming the first African-American president. There was a great deal of optimism regarding all that his presidency would bring.

I started work with Schlumberger in Denver in June, and the Democratic National Convention was held in Denver that year. Barack Obama was nominated to run for president on the Democratic ticket. He eventually won the election, and by the time he was sworn in, in January 2009, the economy was almost collapsing.

Oil companies were hit hard, and their response was massive layoffs. Schlumberger laid off fifteen thousand employees to try to stop the bleeding. I was spared during the initial layoffs because we were busy in the Denver office, but as the recession worsened, our activity slowed, and the Denver office began laying off people as well. We were all praying and hoping that my job would be spared.

We had every reason to be concerned; we were expecting our fourth child! I was on an H-1B visa, and if I was not working, I would be out of status. Being out of status meant violating immigration laws and risking deportation.

Our daughter was born in April of that year, and my mother-in-law came to visit us—seven people under one roof. Then the worst happened. The crisis in the oil and gas industry caught up with us, and Schlumberger laid me off. I don't know how I drove home after I got the news, but somehow I did. During the drive home, I could not think nor express any emotions, but when I got home and my wife gave me a hug, we both wept.

After a good cry, we made up our minds to pray and face the situation head on. I called the company and learned that they were willing to pay for my family to relocate to Cameroon as soon as possible, but we were not ready to move back. The person I spoke with reminded me that if I turned down the offer, I would be here in the country on my own. By law, I could not work for another company unless the new company was willing to transfer my H-1B visa to a Green Card. With the economy being in the state that it was, this was not likely.

This was when we decided to move back to Dallas for me to enroll in an MBA degree program at The University of Texas. We chose UT–Dallas for practical reasons. I had just graduated from there, and my transcripts and other documents were still on file. I could easily get recommendation letters and all that was required for me to get into the program.

In May I had proudly graduated and been employed, and here I was only three months later, unemployed and right back in school. Being a student meant changing my visa once again from H-1B back to the F-1 with all its restrictions. I had hoped that being an alumnus of UTD would make it easy for me to get an on-campus job—maybe as a teaching assistant—but things did not go as I had hoped.

Since we were not earning money, I decided to pay my tuition with a credit card. Tuition for an international student was not cheap, and even with a generous scholarship that reduced my fees to the same as in-state, I still had to pay more than eight thousand dollars per semester. By the second semester, I had more than sixteen thousand dollars of debt on my credit card. We realized that this could not continue.

To stop going to school meant that I, my wife, and our son would all be out of status and could be deported. As we contemplated what to do, the same old ideas and advice began pouring in. Some wondered aloud why, after being in the country for over eight years, we still had not solved our paper problems. I found myself explaining once again that I could not and would not declare political asylum, arrange a fake marriage, use someone else's social security number, or any other illegal activity.

I most certainly was not interested in divorcing my wife, marrying someone else, and then divorcing that woman and remarrying my wife after my Green Card is issued! Marriage is sacred, and there was no way we were going to mess with it:

> *Some Pharisees came and tested him by asking, "Is it lawful for a man to divorce his wife?"*
>
> *"What did Moses command you?" he replied.*
>
> *They said, "Moses permitted a man to write a certificate of divorce and send her away."*
>
> *"It was because your hearts were hard that Moses wrote you this law," Jesus replied. "But at the beginning of creation God 'made them male and female.' For this reason a man will leave his father and mother and be united to his wife, and the two will become one flesh. So, they are no longer two, but one flesh. Therefore what God has joined together, let no one separate."(Mark 10:2–9)*

Scripture is clear: what God has joined together, let no immigration situation separate.

The Second F-1 Visa for My Wife

When I went back to school for the MBA, my wife had moved from an H-4 visa back to an F-2, but classes at the university were expensive, and we could not continue digging our debt hole any deeper. By the end of the first semester, we determined that it made more sense for her to go back to college instead of me. She could take credits at the local community college that would enable her to eventually transfer to a four-year school.

We submitted an application to change my wife's visa to F-1, and my son and I were listed as her dependents. This meant we were giving up any possibility of my getting a job. I would become a stay-at-home dad while my wife went to school.

Even though my wife's tuition at the community college was much cheaper than mine was at the university, we continued having to use credit cards to fund her education.

The First F2-Visa for Me: The Cost is Too High; Let Us Consider the EB-2 Visa

The pressure was mounting, and friends kept bugging us to do something about our situation. I was hesitant but eventually caved and sought the help of a lawyer. This particular law firm specialized in immigration law and was highly recommended. After I presented my situation to him, he indicated that there was the possibility I could qualify for the EB-2 visa.[12] This visa is awarded to those who have demonstrated that they have a high level of expertise in their field of specialization (the arts, sciences, and business). My case was not very strong, in my own judgment, but it would not hurt to try.

The first legal consultation had been free, but to continue would require a three-thousand-dollar deposit. My wife and I decided we would use part of the severance pay I had received from Schlumberger to pay the attorney's and application fees. He gave me a list of requirements to be fulfilled, and one of them was to get recommendations from prominent members of society who would attest to my contribution. I was excited at the possibility of getting a Green Card after many years of waiting.

---

[12] The EB 2 Visa, also referred to as the Employment Based Immigration: Second Preferred, is issued to foreign professionals with advanced degrees in their professions.

CHAPTER SEVEN

DV Lottery: The Good, the Bad, and the Ugly

I heard about the United States Diversity Visa program[13] while I was still an undergraduate in Cameroon. Back then, we were not well informed about the merits of the program or how to participate. We were told that the US was looking for people to send to areas that are sparsely populated, and Alaska was one of those places. Some even went further, emphasizing that you forfeit your freedom when you win the Diversity Visa because the government will force you to live anywhere and ask you do whatever it wants. According to some, this was a sort of modern slavery. None of this information was true, but at the time I

---

[13] The Diversity Immigrant Visa program is a United States congressionally mandated lottery program for receiving a United States Permanent Resident Card. It is also known as the Green Card Lottery.

did not know any better, so in spite of all my doubts, I went ahead and mailed in an entry. And with each passing year, as I became more familiar with the rules and regulations of the program, I continued making entries.

Twelve years after I'd first heard of the program, I was living in Dallas with my family and could not get a job because of the economic downturn and the lack of a work permit. Since no one was willing to hire me without a permit, we considered going back to Cameroon but concluded that it was not yet time. I told my wife we should pray and ask God to put the Green Card in the mail for us. I reasoned that if God wanted us to live in the United States, He would provide for us to stay in the country legally. I knew that would only be possible by our acquiring permanent resident status.

I wondered how such a thing would come to pass. When was God going to come through for us? All these questions and many others ran through my mind. We made our thirteenth entry that year and waited. The entry was made in October, and we declared a month-long fast in January. We prayed about many things but mainly for our immigration situation. We needed a way out, but there was little we could do.

In May, I succumbed to pressure from friends and went to see a lawyer. About a week after I paid the law firm three thousand dollars to file an application for an exceptional ability visa, I received a phone call that changed my life forever.

I was away from home when my cell phone rang. My wife, on the end of the line, told me to hold my breath.

I asked her, "What's the matter? Is everything okay? Did somebody call from Cameroon? Are the children okay?"

She replied, "There's nothing wrong. I have good news. You won the DV lottery!"

I said, "No way!" Back then the results were sent out of Kentucky by mail, so when my wife said I had an email from Kentucky, my first response was that this might be a scam. (It is not unusual for scammers to send fake emails to people telling them they have won the Diversity Visa lottery with the intention of defrauding them.)

I told my wife that I was not going to fall for a scam. I asked her, "Are you sure the email is not fake?" She said the email looked legitimate. I still was not convinced, so I asked her to tell me if the email ended with ".gov." She told me that the email indeed ended with ".gov."

This was too good to be true! I told the person I was with that I had to go back home and verify that I had won the DV lottery. When I got home, I called immediately, and it was confirmed that I had in fact won! The notification had been mailed to a wrong address, and the mail had been returned, which is why they had decided to contact me through email.

I dropped the phone and hugged my wife, and together we wept. These were tears of joy and relief for we knew firsthand that we were witnessing a miracle.[14] God was answering our prayers. We had persevered, and

---

[14] That year more than fifteen million people applied for fifty thousand visas, and I got one of them. I had applied every year for thirteen years.

now we were reaping a good return. Our lives were about to change for the better.

Permanent Resident Card (Green Card)

Now that we had won the DV, it was time to change our visas to permanent residency, a process that would span the next nine months. In the DV lottery, selection is a two-step process. Out of the one hundred thousand people selected initially, only fifty thousand will be issued Green Cards. For that reason, some people who are among the one hundred thousand will never get a Green Card; they have to make the cut.

The DV results were released towards the end of May, about a week after I had paid the first installment of the lawyer's fees to apply for an EB-2 visa. When I got the results, I immediately went to my lawyer's office and told him that I had won the DV and would no longer need his services. I asked that the three thousand dollars be returned to me. A few days later, I received an invoice justifying how the three thousand dollars had already been spent.

This did not make sense, but the joy of having won the DV consoled us. We kept wondering how the law firm could do this to us. We were experiencing deep financial difficulties. Neither of us was earning any money at the time, and coming up with three thousand dollars had truly been an act of desperation—like a drowning person who would grab the tail of a snake if he thought it would save him.

We resolved to let bygones be bygones. We had to forget this incident with the immigration lawyers and move on. There was a long and costly journey ahead of us, and we didn't need to be distracted by the money we had just lost.

This incident did teach me a lesson though. When faced with difficulty, choose your counselors wisely. I had failed to follow my own convictions and instead went with my friend's advice, and it cost me three thousand dollars! If I had waited just one more week, the story would have been entirely different.

Medical Exam and Vaccinations

One of the requirements of applying for permanent residency was a comprehensive medical exam for which we paid out of pocket since we did not have insurance. After completing the exam, the doctor put the results in an envelope, sealed it, and handed it to us to include as part of the application package. We had to have a TB test, the results of which were included in the application as well. And finally, we had to be current on our vaccinations. On top of the medical exam, TB test, and vaccinations, we were required to pay an application fee of more than fifteen hundred dollars per person. This was an astronomical amount to a family in dire financial straits.

Because the process is lengthy and costly, some of the people who are selected through the DV lottery never make it to the US. In fact, the year we were selected, one of our friends still living in Cameroon was also selected but could not make it because she could not afford the cost involved.

About six months after winning the DV, we figured, based on projections on the Department of Homeland Security's website, that we were about three months away from having our application processed. We were wrong. We had mailed in our application along with more than thirty-five hundred dollars in application fees, and in a few months the whole package, minus the cashier's check, was sent back to us! Their reason for rejecting our application was simply that we had sent it in too early. We were instructed to reapply and pay new application fees. Wow!

We had no choice but to pay the application fees a second time. This truly was tough for us financially, but we had to get the process done—and done correctly. Next, we were required to have fingerprinting done and then go in for an interview with an immigration official to ensure that we were who we claimed to be. We were placed under oath to respond truthfully. We had to ensure that we had come here and remained here legally, and that we had not been involved in any criminal activity. The interview was successful since we, of course, had nothing to hide.

While waiting for the Green Card to be issued, I had applied for a temporary work permit—which was granted—but I still could not get a job with it because of the slowdown in the oil and gas industry. To say that we were excited when my Green Card finally arrived is an understatement. It had taken almost ten years of waiting and jumping through bureaucratic hoops, but at last we were permanent residents of the United States of America!

We had been ridiculed and misunderstood because we refused to do what others were doing, but our greatest joy was that we had done it the right way.

Armed with the permanent resident card, I was ready to go visit my parents in Cameroon. Up until this point, I had not traveled out of the country. I could not wait to see my mother again and to hug her. I had not seen my parents, siblings, extended family, and friends in more than nine years. My entire family was waiting for me when I arrived at the airport. My younger sister welcomed me with a song, together with my nieces and nephews whom I was meeting for the very first time.

I felt a peace and calmness that words cannot describe as I slept in the same old bed I had slept in growing up. My mother and father were so pleased and proud to see me. During my month-long stay in Cameroon, I visited a lot of people and places. Everywhere I went people welcomed me with open arms, excitement, and a lot of questions. How was the United States? What type of food do you eat there? Can you eat Cameroonian food there? How is the weather? How many children do you have? Do your children speak Mundani? When are they coming to visit? Did you miss us? The questions were endless.

The reunion was magnificent, and while my heart was filled with gratitude, the cost and sacrifice of having been away for so long hit me hard. A lot had transpired. Many people whom I loved had died and were buried without my attending their funerals. There were nephews, nieces, and cousins whom I did not recognize. The adults had grown older, and the kids were now adults with their own children. Had the high cost of leaving my country for a foreign land been worth it?

The first time I traveled to the States, it had been on a non-immigrant student visa. I had thought that after graduating I would work for a few years then come back home, but as the end of my Cameroonian visit drew nearer, it dawned on me that it was time for me to move forward. America was going to be my new home. I was certain that my destiny—all that I was created to accomplish—was tied directly to the United States of America.

The bottom line is this: we are not our own, and God has the right to send us on assignment to any part of the world. The entire globe is the Lord's, and He knows the best place for us to live and where we can have maximum impact on his kingdom and glory. In our case, God had confirmed that America was the place for us to settle, and we were willing to follow the will of God regardless of the cost.

I called together all of my family in Cameroon and asked them to pray for me. I knelt, and my family prayed for me and released me to come back to the United States to establish my permanent home. This was more precious than anything they could have given me. Up to this point, I had twice offered up on the altar my dream of living in America, and through Divine intervention God had arranged for us to stay. This time I was coming back to America with a strong sense of purpose, determination, and excitement knowing God has something wonderful in store for me and my family.

CHAPTER EIGHT

US Citizenship: Victory at Last

I came back from Cameroon and started my tenth year in the US. In another five years, I could become a United States citizen. These five years promised to be not nearly as challenging and difficult as the past ten had been because now we were permanent residents. Four years into a new, full-time job with benefits, I was once again laid off, but this time I did not panic. Having that permanent residence permit made a world of difference in how we handled the situation.

About this same time, we submitted our application to become US citizens. The process required us to submit biometric information (fingerprinting), pay for the change of status, pass a citizenship exam, and demonstrate that we could read and write basic English. After we checked all these boxes, all that was left was to attend the swearing-in ceremony where we would become naturalized citizens.

Having waited fourteen years and a few days, at last the time came for me, my wife, and my son to become citizens of the United States of America. That day was September 2, 2016. The entire family went to the courthouse in downtown Dallas for the swearing-in ceremony. It was a bittersweet day for me because Cameroon, the country of my birth, does not allow dual citizenship. Becoming an American citizen meant I had to give up my Cameroonian citizenship. In the future, whenever I wanted to visit Cameroon, I would have to apply for a visa to enter the country. Despite the requirements, I willfully chose to become a citizen of the United States of America. The boundless opportunities this country affords outweigh all that I was giving up.

People from thirty-nine different countries and every continent participated in the ceremony. Proudly, we took the naturalization oath of allegiance to the United States of America:

> "I hereby declare, on oath, that I absolutely and entirely renounce and abjure all allegiance and fidelity to any foreign prince, potentate, state, or sovereignty, of whom or which I have heretofore been a subject or citizen; that I will support and defend the Constitution and laws of the United States of America against all enemies, foreign and domestic; that I will bear true faith and allegiance to the same; that I will bear arms on behalf of the United States when required by the law; that I will perform noncombatant service in the Armed Forces

> of the United States when required by the law; that I will perform work of national importance under civilian direction when required by the law; and that I take this obligation freely, without any mental reservation or purpose of evasion; so help me God."

It was such a beautiful and moving ceremony. Many memories flooded my mind as I sat in the courtroom waiting for my naturalization certificate. It felt almost as if it was not really happening, but it was. The long road to American citizenship was nearing its end, and we had persevered and overcome. I found myself overwhelmed with gratitude for all the people who had helped us along the way. All I could say was thank you, Lord; thank you, Lord. I was experiencing one of the greatest experiments in human history—that is, people from all different backgrounds coming together to form a country, united by a common desire for freedom, liberty, and justice for all.

The next phase of my journey was about to begin. I was being given the opportunity to find my place—to leave my mark on the history of this nation just as millions have done before me. I felt the weight of responsibility that comes with being a citizen of this great country. Becoming an American citizen is about more than its privileges and benefits; it is about moving the country to the next level, leaving it better than we found it, and ensuring that the freedoms we have are preserved for the next generation.

The Pledge of Allegiance has a special meaning to me now that I have become a citizen. Each time I recite it, I think of the sacrifices made by all those who came before me. The Founding Fathers placed all on the line for an ideal that many considered unattainable, and they risked all to realize it. Since then, many have followed in the footsteps of our founding fathers at great personal cost— even the ultimate sacrifice of losing their lives—to defend the freedoms we now enjoy. That is why after my swearing-in ceremony I posted the following statement on all my social media sites:

> "Today is the greatest day of my life. I am finally a US citizen after 14 yrs. America is truly the greatest country on Earth, and I am proud and honored to join the millions who have gone before me to maintain her greatness. There are few places on earth that somebody can show up with a single suitcase, without money, and make it. America has been extremely good to me. She is not perfect, but there is a lot of goodness to her, and now is the time to participate in bringing solutions to some of her challenges. I am thrilled at this opportunity."

The response on LinkedIn, one of the premier professional networking platforms, was swift and amazing. I received more than twenty-nine thousand "likes" and more than three thousand comments. Nearly all of the comments were positive, uplifting, and celebratory. The support and encouragement poured in for days, and more than a thousand people "connected" with me. What I learned from this is that doing the right thing—even when it is difficult and unpopular—will eventually pay off. People will support you, applaud you, and respect you when you stand your ground and allow character, integrity, and moral rectitude—rather than your circumstances—inform your choices.

The following is a sampling of comments I received from Americans representing all walks of life, religious and political affiliation, gender, and ethnicity. I obtained permission from each individual to reprint their posts as written. The only changes were in the case of glaring grammatical errors:

> "Because of your love and appreciation for people and country you are already an American. A truer American than many who were born into it . . . Best wishes for your future." —Christopher S.
>
> "This is precisely the problem with America. It makes its most qualified and skilled residents who study and stay here contribute to taxes, innovation, and big corporate profits, but makes them wait 14 years for a right to vote and be a citizen?? Open your eyes people; the US is the land of opportunity but also the land of exploitation. Give people rights sooner, and they will be more patriotic and loyal!" —Sonal D., MBA

"14 years? Any wonder we have so many undocumented foreigners living in the US?" —Jim K., LCPC, CSADC

"You sir, are the kind of immigrant this country desperately needs. Welcome to the most exceptional country on the planet!" —Eli H.

"Congratulations! I hope someday those of us who were born here can learn to appreciate the opportunities that are here for us as you do. Your spirit and gratitude are beautiful!" —Rena D.

"CONGRATULATIONS!!! We are happy to welcome you especially since you followed the protocol (laws) in becoming a citizen. Thank you for sharing your experience. I wish you happiness and much success!" —Susan R.

"You are what America is all about. We want people to come here and LOVE our country and be happy to be here. I was born an American as were my parents. I am so proud and grateful for the gift of being an American, and I am glad to hear that you [are too]. Thank you for sharing your story, and I wish you much success! Congratulations and welcome once again from one proud American to another!" — Donna C., CPA, CGMA, ACE

> "Fixing immigration would start with changing 14 years to 14 days, wouldn't it?" —Bill E.

> "Congratulations and welcome home! Thank you for sharing your story and for being a positive example of how to immigrate legally. It's great to call you a fellow American!" —Braxton B.

> "Eric, welcome aboard! As a recruiter, I know this process can be an arduous one. I salute you on respecting the laws of this nation and putting in the effort to become one of us. Congratulations!" —Keith R.

> "We welcome you with open arms... because you did it legally! This day you are one of US." —Jeff D.

> "Welcome to this country. Great to see you had the moral and ethical backbone to respect the laws of a country you so love and decided to do it the right way." —John M., MBA, PharmD

> "This is fabulous! Welcome US citizen. I helped a friend study for this test and knew that it was difficult. A lot of Americans could not answer those questions. Kudos to you." —Dr. Sandra F.

> "You will truly bring value to our country as a citizen and as an American because you like most of us born Americans have had to understand our bill of rights and constitution. Congratulations on being an American and a citizen of the United States of America!" —Tina D.

The response to my post was overwhelming and breathtaking, and overall the comments were supportive and encouraging. (One person called me the N-word for celebrating my American citizenship.) Most people just typed congratulations. Those who wrote more praised me for doing it the right way.

Based on the comments, most Americans are not against immigration; they are against illegal immigration. There are thousands of people inside and outside of the United States who believe in the rule of law and are waiting patiently for their turn to become part of this great country. These people ought not to be treated as the enemy.

CHAPTER NINE

The Discussion that We as a Country Need to Have

Because you are still reading this book, I know the issue of immigration is important to you and that you desire to make a difference. I am inviting you now to put on your solutions hat and let us look for answers.

Before we dive into solutions, however, we need to take a quick look at why people immigrate. You may be wondering why in the world I would put my family through all that you have just read about. Why would I not just go back to Cameroon, my country of origin? The simple answer is, "The American Dream." I lived in America long enough to get a taste of the opportunities available to me in this, the greatest country on Earth.

For most people across the globe, the place they currently occupy is not where their ancestors originated. Migration has, is, and always will be part of the human experience, and here is why:

Lack of Economic Opportunities

When economic conditions are not favorable, people pack up their belongings and move. In Cameroon, I had graduated with a master's degree in geology but I was jobless, so when the opportunity to go to graduate school in the US presented itself, I seized it. Each year, thousands of international students arrive on the US shore in the quest for better education, jobs, and an improved economic outlook.

Immigrants would do well to come into the country resolved to do all that is within their power to improve the economy. Learning English and other skills that will position them to take full advantage of the country's economic opportunities should be encouraged. Participating in the socio-political life of the country and making their voice heard on important issues is crucial. Why come this far to settle for less? When immigrants learn to fit in and get assimilated, everyone wins. Those advocating for immigrants to maintain their old ways and not become integrated into mainstream America are doing the immigrants and their families a disservice, encouraging them to sacrifice their future economic freedom, earnings, and purchasing power on the altar of comfort.

The lure of the familiar and the comfortable is extremely strong. Immigrants can allow fear to keep them from discovering, developing, and deploying their full potential. They ought to be reminded that being a part of America's melting pot does not mean losing their identity, but rather adding their own "flavor" and making it "taste" better—making their new country better than the one they left behind.

Freedom

It is the quest for freedom that propels a baby to be delivered. After nine months, he decides it is time to leave the confines of his limited space. Part of the reason I left Cameroon, my country of birth, was the desire to be free as well.

The situation in Cameroon is pathetic. The president has been in office since I was in second grade, and there is no indication that he is going to relinquish power anytime soon. The constitution of the country has been changed by the president a couple of times to benefit him and not the country. The last change was to eliminate presidential term limits so he can remain in office.

The president has absolute power. Supreme Court justices, governors, lawmakers, chancellors, deans, and department heads at state universities—all are appointed or removed by the president without the approval of parliament.

The president has been able to maintain an iron grip on the country by perpetuating a culture of fear and intimidation. He selects a few individuals who are beholden to him, and these elites are beneficiaries of the system and proxies of the man in power. During elections, the president has them campaign in their assigned regions on his behalf. The campaigns usually focus on the personality of the president, not the issues.

When I was an undergraduate student, one of my uncles, a high-ranking government official, demanded that I campaign on behalf of the ruling party, but I refused. I would not toe the line for a hypocritical government that pretends to be for the people but is more interested in maintaining power at any cost.

The suffering of the masses means nothing to the government. There is little being done to strengthen the democratic institution because it is impossible to concentrate power in the hands of a single individual and have strong institutions and the rule of law at the same time. I was fed up with the system and vowed I would never work for the Cameroonian government.

Dictatorial regimes lead to the abuse of power and the misuse of natural resources, depriving most of its citizens of basic necessities such as food, shelter, and housing. People are persecuted and some even lose their lives because of their political and religious beliefs. Millions have escaped these dictatorial regimes to places they have heard people can be free to speak their minds, practice the religion of their choosing, and hold any beliefs without interference by the government.

America is one of such places, and over the years millions have immigrated here because the constitution guarantees freedom and the pursuit of happiness. In America one has the ability to speak his mind without fear of arrest and detention. That is why when the opportunity to leave Cameroon for America presented itself, I jumped on it. Here I am free to write a book of this nature and express my ideas without fear of reprisal.

The Founding Fathers of the United States of America risked their lives to declare independence from the British empire. They boldly declared:

> "We hold these Truths to be self-evident, that all Men are created equal, that they are endowed by their Creator with certain unalienable Rights, that among these are Life, Liberty, and the pursuit of Happiness. That to secure these Rights, Governments are instituted among Men, deriving their just Powers from the Consent of the Governed, that whenever any Form of Government becomes destructive of these Ends, it is the Right of the People to alter or abolish it, and to institute new Government, laying its Foundation on such Principles, and organizing its Powers in such Form, as to them shall seem most likely to effect their Safety and Happiness."

The spirit behind the Declaration of Independence is alive and well. This declaration is one of the most powerful in all of human history, and it is important that we pay close attention. We are not the result of some random, purposeless mutation; we are created by a Creator, and this Creator—not the government—gives us certain rights that cannot be taken away or denied. Because we are all created, we are all equal.

Unfortunately, most governments in the world are established for those in power, not for the people. Some of these governments have taken the place of the Creator, resulting in a society like the one described in George Orwell's *Animal Farm*: "All animals are equal, but some are more equal than others."[15] These governments believe that all humans are equal, but some are more equal than others. If government is the giver and guarantor of our rights, government can take away these rights whenever they deem it necessary. This is why people are not free to pursue happiness and liberty in many countries of the world—because a few individuals who see themselves as the smart and wise elites have taken the entire country hostage.

The appeal of a government that takes care of its citizens is attractive until you realize that the government is not a supernatural being. The government is made up of individuals who have an agenda and can make terrible mistakes. Our Founding Fathers understood firsthand the dangers of allowing government to become unaccountable to the people. We have three separate branches of government to ensure that there are checks and balances and that power is not abused. So far this has worked, but we the people must consciously be on the watch, and if the government at any point tries to become the creator and the issuer of our fundamental, unalienable rights, we the people should dissolve that government. This statement would be considered treasonous in most countries of the world; the people have no right whatsoever to topple the government. No wonder dictators are running amok, and

---

[15] George Orwell, *Animal Farm* (London: Secker and Warburg, 1945).

millions of people have been deprived of their fundamental rights of assembly, freedom of speech, and expression.

America is still the land of the free and the home of the brave, and her exceptionalism cannot be disputed. All who immigrate here because they want to be free must understand that freedom is never given, but taken. They must be reminded that the freedoms we enjoy in this country came at a price, and all are expected to uphold these freedoms and keep the United States of America the shining city on a hill that many oppressed people all over the world can run to when they can no longer bear the yoke of oppression.

Conquest

Conquest is using force to displace people and occupy their land. This has been an integral part of human history, although we are getting a little better at keeping our hands off other people's lands. That being said, people still immigrate today with the intention of conquering other lands. At times, the strategy used is not military but the spreading of ideas that will eventually undermine the values and customs of the country to which they have immigrated. This is why it is legitimate for any country to ask those desiring to enter what their intentions are. A country has the right to defend its sovereignty at all costs.

Until the day countries and national boundaries cease to exist, every country has the right and obligation to protect its national borders and protect its citizens. Unfortunately, the same people advocating for borderless states live behind secured fences. Why is a fence necessary if free mobility of people is the acceptable standard?

Forceful Relocation

Slavery is the perfect example of forceful relocation. People are captured, sold, and carried away from their country of origin to a different country without their consent. The impact of such an act is far-reaching, and America is still dealing with the ramifications of the transatlantic slave trade. Millions of Africans were sold to Europeans who transported them to the Carribean, South America, and North America to work on plantations under inhumane conditions. This dark page in our history should not be swept under the rug. Healing and restoration will be achieved when the country comes to terms with her past by accepting that an atrocious crime was committed and acknowledging this wrong.

Sex slavery and human trafficking are still rampant all over the world today. Children are being taken from rural areas to cities and subjected to harsh working conditions by their masters and mistresses. This is slavery under the guise of employment, and it must be stopped at all costs.

People emigrate all the time in search of better conditions. The big questions are why do we have failed systems? Why do some places lack economic opportunities? Why in some places is there no freedom of expression? The short answer to all these whys is rooted in failure by humans to live by the Golden Rule—that is, to do unto others as they would have others do unto them.

Most countries have laws that the rich and powerful break with impunity. Many governments bite off more than they can chew, and the result is waste, mismanagement, corruption, and nepotism. In such countries, the ruling elite uses fear and intimidation to subject and oppress people. Any opposing voices are shut down by the police and military. At the head of such governments are dictators who are worshiped almost as gods. They create the impression that the country will perish without them. In short, they weaken the institutions of the country, and there is no separation of power. This one man makes the entire country believe that he is the best thing that ever happened to them. To move ahead, you must sing the praise of those in power.

I refused to sing the praises of those in power and advocated that the government should be the referee instead of "Santa" with a big bag, handing out goodies especially during elections. That is why when I came to the United States I obeyed the law and toed the line. Breaking laws leads to a broken system. If we have laws on the books, they must be obeyed. No one motivated by political or personal gain should advocate or encourage other people to break the law.

I and most others who have moved to the United States know that when laws are broken the system will not work well, and the result will be anarchy. When laws are broken, everybody including the lawbreakers will be affected, and the system will eventually collapse on itself.

According to some estimates, as many as fifteen million people may be in the United States illegally. We may go about our day-to-day activities as if nothing is happening, or we can learn more about the plight of illegal immigrants and do something about it. Saying the problem of illegal immigration is too complex is not an excuse for inaction; therefore, in the next chapter, I propose three solutions.

CHAPTER TEN

The Way Forward

With upwards of fifteen million undocumented aliens living in the United States, it is time that we find solutions to stop illegal immigration. But to find any lasting solution requires that we accurately define the problem. First, who ought to be considered an immigrant and who ought not to be considered an immigrant? How can somebody who was issued a non-immigrant visa to come and visit the US become an immigrant? How can somebody who crossed the border and entered the US illegally become an immigrant? What about the person who was admitted into the country on a temporary non- immigrant work visa? Contrary to what some believe, declaring oneself an immigrant does not make him one. Until our laws are changed, someone who obtains a non- immigrant visa to visit the US cannot suddenly become an immigrant.

A person who sneaks into the country without proper documentation cannot claim to be an immigrant either. I am not against people moving freely and settling wherever they wish and doing whatever they want, but unfortunately, every country in the world has immigration laws that are enforced. Those trying to hold America to a different standard are being disingenuous. Most of them come from countries that do not even have a path to citizenship for people from other parts of the world. And even if they did, outsiders would have a hard time fitting in because of ethnic divisions that are prevalent in these countries.

It is said that people who live in glass houses should not throw stones. Many people currently living in the United States are quick to condemn the US for being too restrictive with its immigration policies while forgetting that their former home countries have draconian immigration laws in place as well. For example, in most countries being born there does not guarantee citizenship, but a child born in the US is considered a citizen immediately, regardless of the immigration status of the parents. That is why so many people take advantage of the United States and have "anchor babies" here.

Only after I moved to the United States and experienced the inconveniences of living in a foreign country without proper documentation did I begin to understand what immigrants were going through in Cameroon, my own country of origin. Children born in Cameroon to parents from other countries are not automatically considered Cameroonian. When these children grow up and apply to attend state universities, their tuition is usually close to twenty times higher than that of Cameroonian students.

There are many Nigerians living and working in Cameroon, but just like in America, they have restrictions on them. They cannot vote in any elections, and it is impossible for them to work for the government. They are required to pay for a resident permit on an annual basis and are required to carry proof of residency with them at all times. The Cameroonian law enforcement officials are well known for intercepting public transportation buses to enforce these laws. Nigerians and other foreigners who do not have proof of permanent residency are forced off the buses, and money is accepted from them in the form of bribes.

While I lived in Cameroon, I never saw anyone on the streets demonstrating on behalf of foreigners living there. There was no effort to open the Cameroonian borders and let in whoever wants to come. In fact, over the years the Nigerian government has deported many Cameroonians for various reasons. The South African government has done the same. There is no way a person can travel to Australia, China, Japan, or any European country without a valid visa. When you move to any of these countries, you must toe the line or be deported. I point this out to highlight the fact that the movement of people across the globe is controlled and restricted by all countries, and America should not be vilified for applying the same common sense.

All of us will agree that proper planning and management of resources is crucial for sustainability, safety, and the welfare of all. Imagine getting up one morning and driving your child to a school that was built to hold three hundred students but has two thousand students waiting to get in. The chaos that would ensue if demand were suddenly to overwhelm supply is something we must do all to avoid. When things are done in an orderly and organized fashion, everyone benefits.

The world is more connected than most realize. What happens in one part of the globe has the potential to affect all of us, no matter where we live. Being our brother's keeper has never been so urgent and necessary. We live in a time of high connectivity, and people all over the world only have to look on Google Earth to see what is behind all those high walls. In the past, information took months, if not years, to travel the globe; now it is instantaneous. Children in the remotest parts of the world can connect to the internet and see what type of classrooms and resources are being used by their peers in more affluent societies. The pressure to have these advancements and modernizations is mounting and must be dealt with. We have to challenge ourselves to think outside the box to come up with solutions that make sense and are achievable.

America's Founding Fathers believed and clearly stated that all men are created equal, with inalienable rights endowed by their Creator. Contained in this rich Judeo- Christian heritage are principles that have made and will keep America great if she will continue to operate in accordance with them. Some of our nation's leaders, such as Martin Luther King, Jr., who championed the civil rights movement, were Christians who allowed the Bible to inform their sense of right and wrong. As we navigate through the complexities of our current immigration challenge, the Bible still offers much needed moral clarity. After all, the Bible is the inspired, inerrant word of God, and we can depend on it for moral direction. Here are some of its teachings:

> *And you are to love those who are foreigners, for you yourselves were foreigners in Egypt. (Deuteronomy 10:19)*
>
> *Keep on loving one another as brothers and sisters. Do not forget to show hospitality to strangers, for by so doing some people have shown hospitality to angels without knowing it. (Hebrews 13:1–2)*

Most of us are aware of the Golden Rule:

> *So, in everything, do to others what you would have them do to you, for this sums up the Law and the Prophets. (Mathew 7:12)*

Based on the Golden Rule, what is good for you is good for others as well; therefore, we must be considerate of others no matter who they are or where they come from. We must treat people with dignity, respect, and honor, for that is how we would like to be treated. In addition to being fair and honest with others, we must extend love, mercy, and compassion to strangers—that is, to non-immigrants, immigrants, and illegal immigrants. Love is crucial in our interaction with one another. A teacher of the law trying to figure out the best way to please God posed the following question to Jesus Christ:

> *Teacher, which is the greatest commandment in the Law?*
>
> Jesus replied: *"Love the Lord your God with all your heart and with all your soul and with all your mind." This is the first and greatest commandment. And the second is like it: "Love your neighbor as yourself." All the Law and the Prophets hang on these two commandments. (Mathew 22:36–40)*

The statement Jesus made is extremely important. All we need is to love God and love our neighbor, and all will be well. What does it mean to love God and love our neighbor? First, we have to understand what love is.

> *Dear friends, let us love one another, for love comes from God. Everyone who loves has been born of God and knows God. Whoever does not love does not know God, because God is love. This is how God showed his love among us: He sent his one and only Son into the world that we might live through him. This is love: not that we loved God, but that he loved us and sent his Son as an atoning sacrifice for our sins. Dear friends, since God so loved us, we also ought to love one another. No one has ever seen God; but if we love one another, God lives in us and his love is made complete in us. This is how we*

> *know that we live in him and he in us: He has given us of his Spirit. And we have seen and testify that the Father has sent his Son to be the Savior of the world. If anyone acknowledges that Jesus is the Son of God, God lives in them and they in God. And so we know and rely on the love God has for us. God is love. Whoever lives in love lives in God, and God in them. (1 John 4:7–16)*

To truly love, we need God, for it is only when we have God that we can love as He loves. His is a redeeming love. It is a giving love that takes initiative, that makes the first move. God loves people, and to love Him is to love people. We have to be missional in our approach to God's kind of love. Loving people does not mean letting them do whatever they want; it means pointing them to Jesus, the true source of love, so that they might be reconciled to God.

A proper understanding of the love of God will enable us to have a balanced view of God's nature and expectations. There are specific instructions in the Bible concerning our attitude towards authority:

> *Submit yourselves for the Lord's sake to every human authority: whether to the emperor, as the supreme authority, or to governors, who are sent by him to punish those who do wrong and to commend those who do right. For it is God's will that by doing good you should silence the ignorant talk of foolish people. Live as free people,*

> *but do not use your freedom as a cover-up for evil; live as God's slaves. Show proper respect to everyone, love the family of believers, fear God, honor the emperor. (1 Peter 2:13–17 NIV)*

Our love for God is made evident through our obedience to him. We cannot say we love God and disobey His commandments. We are to obey governing authorities not only to escape punishment but also to serve as an example to others. The following passage by Paul the apostle stresses the need to obey governing authorities:

> *Let everyone be subject to the governing authorities, for there is no authority except that which God has established. The authorities that exist have been established by God. Consequently, whoever rebels against the authority is rebelling against what God has instituted, and those who do so will bring judgment on themselves. For rulers hold no terror for those who do right, but for those who do wrong. Do you want to be free from fear of the one in authority? Then do what is right, and you will be commended. For the one in authority is God's servant for your good. But if you do wrong, be afraid, for rulers do not bear the sword for no reason. They are God's servants, agents of wrath to bring punishment on the wrongdoer.*

> *Therefore, it is necessary to submit to the authorities, not only because of possible punishment but also as a matter of conscience. This is also why you pay taxes, for the authorities are God's servants, who give their full time to governing. Give to everyone what you owe them: if you owe taxes, pay taxes; if revenue, then revenue; if respect, then respect; if honor, then honor.*
> *(Romans 13:1–7)*

We cannot in good conscience encourage those who are living in the United States illegally and who are knowingly breaking federal immigration laws to continue to do so. If everybody made a habit of breaking laws because they believed the laws do not favor them, our society would break down and become chaotic. There is nothing evil or immoral about the United States immigration laws, but that does not mean there is no room for improvement or adjustments to be made.

So far I have narrated my own personal experience regarding the US immigration system and why I chose not to become an illegal alien. My decision was not influenced by how difficult or unfair the United States immigration laws are nor by what others were doing. Rather, my decisions and my moral compass were based wholly on God's Word. I understood that to be a person of integrity, I must hold myself to a higher standard, and this standard requires speaking the truth and doing what is right even when conditions are not right.

Maybe you are thinking that my morals are not for everybody, and I should not impose them on others; you are right. We all have a free will and make choices daily. But there are laws that govern us, and the outcome of our lives is a result of the choices we make. The law of reaping and sowing is one-hundred percent reliable.

The way forward for us as a country is to sit down and figure out the best thing to do, realizing that we need love, mercy, and compassion if we want lasting solutions. That is why I am proposing the following three possible solutions to resolve the present immigration dilemma:

Do Nothing

Doing nothing is the most appealing option to some politicians and citizens, and thus the country has gone down this road for more than two decades with predicable results. Unfortunately, the assumption that if you ignore a problem long enough it will go away only results in the can being kicked down the road for future generations to deal with. In the short run, this solution appears to be the easiest, but the ramifications are quite serious and far reaching.

There are millions of would-be taxpayers living in the shadows of society. They have kids and unfortunately cannot participate in raising them like other families are doing. The fear of deportation keeps them away from PTA meetings and other social gatherings, so if their children are struggling in school, it will be difficult to intervene promptly. As a result, some will drop out of school, and their full potential will not be realized. They may end up depending on the government to take care of them. We as a country cannot afford to kick this can down to the next generation. It is in our best interest to ensure that everybody living here has equal access to resources that will help them maximize their potential. When everybody is functioning at full capacity, the entire nation benefits.

We cannot continue pretending the issue does not exist. All the undocumented illegal aliens in the country are people with hopes, dreams, and ambitions. They too would like to participate in shaping and moving the country forward. They too would like the opportunity to get good-paying jobs and raise their children without fear of being deported.

Refusing to do something about all the illegal aliens in the country is giving legitimacy to all the businesses that employ and exploit illegal aliens. Many of these people, because they have no legal status, cannot take their exploiters to court. They cannot complain when their working conditions are bad or when they are required to work long hours with little pay. We as a society cannot afford to allow such abuse and exploitation to continue.

It makes economic sense for businesses to use cheap labor provided by illegal aliens, but because the workers have no medical insurance and their employers are not required by law to provide any, when these workers become sick and need medical attention, it is not the businesses but the taxpayers who are forced to pay their medical bills. In other words, these business owners are making a profit at the expense of the general public.

The desire to make a profit should not cause us to turn a blind eye to this plight that is plaguing our country. We cannot afford to allow the situation to remain as is. Now is the time to do something, and we should not allow partisan politics and personal interests to prevent us from doing what is right. It is incumbent on us to address these problems, and address it we should!

Deport All the Illegal Immigrants

I hear this one a lot. People make it sound as easy as pie. Just round up all these millions of people—some of which may have lived here for more than twenty years— and send them back to where they came from. Deportation may sound simple, but you have to take into consideration that some of these illegal immigrants have kids who are American citizens and will need their parents to raise them. Some will suggest then that entire families be deported in order to keep them together. The kids who are American citizens can be raised outside the country, and when they become adults, they can move back to the United States without their parents. This is not a good idea; you do not solve a problem by creating another. It is not the fault of the kids that their parents came to the United States illegally. These children are citizens and have the right to be raised in the country of their birth.

We should consider deportation carefully and move cautiously, or we will do more harm than good. Deporting illegal aliens who have committed violent crimes and who are a threat to society should be non- negotiable. But those whose only crime is breaking federal immigration laws should be given a chance to mend their ways, especially if they are willing to satisfy the requirements. If they refuse to do what they are asked to do—for example, to learn English and to wait their turn to become legal immigrants—they would automatically disqualify themselves and be deported. At least under this plan they will have been given a chance but decided not to make the best of it. In that case, they would have only themselves to blame.

Declare Amnesty

A unilateral declaration of amnesty without securing the borders, overhauling the immigration system, and punishing the lawbreakers is an insult to those who are here legally. To some people, giving all illegal aliens a free pass is a loving, caring, and compassionate thing to do. Those advocating this approach talk of fairness and justice; I beg to differ. How is rewarding those who have broken the law justice? What do we tell those who did it the right way at a great personal cost? What about those who have waited for years and are still waiting to do it the right way? Justice requires that all who have broken federal laws pay the penalty. Why is it that American citizens who break federal laws go to jail while illegal aliens who break federal immigration laws go unpunished?

Allowing millions of illegal immigrants to go free is a travesty of justice. If we can incarcerate people for possessing a few grams of marijuana, it is an indication that we take our laws seriously. No one should break the law with impunity and be rewarded. America is strong because no one is above the law; this is not the case in many parts of the world. A strong message has to be sent to would-be immigrants that laws in America have to be respected by everyone at all times.

When people break laws, there is a penalty—either you pay a fine or serve jail time. In the case of illegal immigrants, it is not feasible to jail fifteen million people. The only option is to require illegals to pay a fine, which will place them on a path to permanent residency. Through the process, they will learn to stand in line and wait their turn. If they break the law, they will never become US citizens and will never vote. This would send a strong message.

Any comprehensive immigration plan must start with securing the border. According to Hugh Hewitt, author of *The Fourth Way*, "The fence is the key to the deal, but is not the whole solution as people will continue to overstay visas and human smugglers will continue to cross waters and get in via our ports."[16] I will add that in addition to securing the borders and making it difficult for those who want to come in illegally, there should be a crackdown on those employing illegal aliens. Companies who offer employment to illegal aliens must be dealt heavy fines. This will send a strong message to all business owners to stop this illegal practice. If jobs dry up, the incentive for people to overstay their visas will be taken away, and they will not stay. When people know that paying smugglers large sums of money will not result in job prospects in the United States, they will not risk the trip.

---

[16] Hugh Hewitt, *The Fourth Way*, (New York City: Simon & Schuster, 2017).

A lot of people want to do it right, and they should be encouraged by making the legal immigration process easier. For example, if a student graduates and desires to stay and work in the United States, he should be encouraged to do so by making it easy for him to apply and get permanent residency instead of the H1-B visa that some employers use to offer lower wages.

The solution is definitely not having so-called sanctuary cities. What is a sanctuary city? Do we have a new meaning for the word *sanctuary*? How can a city in a law-abiding country decide to support, finance, and encourage lawlessness and call it sanctuary? And those who speak against this lawlessness are vilified and labeled hateful! People supporting this lawlessness forget that people who are seeking refuge in the United States do it partly because of lawlessness in their own countries. It is shocking that the lives of law-abiding United States citizens living in these so-called sanctuary cities are placed at risk because the mayors prefer to protect criminal aliens. How is this right, just, and honest? It is time to stand up to this distortion of justice. The loving thing to do is to treat everybody fairly and consistently. No one is above the law, and sanctuary cities should be called to order.

Lastly, most people do not move from their countries of origin only because conditions there are not favorable. That is why we must be more globally minded, always looking for ways to empower people to make the most of what they have. This can be done through the private sector and nonprofit organizations. We design sustainable, indigenous-led projects that are owned and managed by locals. We have to move from the model of "we have all the solutions" to working with other stakeholders and incorporating their input.

Thank you so much for sticking with me and reading this book to the end. This is an indication that you care about one of the greatest challenges facing our country and our generation. This is the first step towards finding solutions, and I commend you for taking the time to explore ideas with me. This is just the beginning of the journey. I am counting on you to do all in your power to see that together we come up with a solution. I am a strong believer that knowledge without action is useless. You know you know something when what you know causes you to make changes.

It is often said that the best way to eat an elephant is to take a bite at a time. Do not allow the enormity of this immigration challenge to prevent you from doing something. It is easy to say that others will do something about it, but who are the others? Who knows? Your participation in looking for solutions might be the catalyst that will galvanize the entire country to come up with a solution! You may be saying that now is not the time; I beg to differ. Now is too late. We should have solved this problem more than two decades ago. When President Reagan declared amnesty, our borders were supposed to have been secured, but we failed to do that, and now we are back where we started. This time around, we must do all that we can to get it right, for it is the loving and caring thing to do.

Many illegal aliens move here, and the stress, strain, and inconveniences of being undocumented are disheartening. We can prevent this unnecessary suffering by ensuring that the incentive for them to move here is taken away. The millions of illegal aliens living in the US need to be reached out to. We cannot continue to live as if they do not exist. It is in our best interest to ensure that we get them integrated into society so they can contribute and pay their fair share of taxes. I wrote this book to encourage you to join the conversation about the plight of illegal immigrants and the impact it is having—and will continue to have—on this nation. Call your congressman or congresswoman and the senators representing your state. Email them. Fax them. Do anything you can to ensure that they take up this issue and resolve it. The cost of not doing anything is great. For the sake of the next generation, let your voice be heard.

CHAPTER ELEVEN

An Eternal Perspective

Congratulations! You have done what many people do not. Most people start books and never finish reading them. Yet you persevered, and now you are here.

There is a place that cannot be compared to the USA you don't need a visa to visit or green card to live there. The streets are made out of gold and there is no more death, sorrow and lack there. For you to go there all you need is to become a child of God.

There is nothing more important than being a child of God. I would be wicked if I did not share this truth with you. It is one of the most important things that you will ever do. It is more important than taking care of your physical body because your body will eventually decay. While you mustn't damage your body through drinking sugar, your body will eventually die. But there is a part of your that is more important. This is your spirit because it is eternal. Therefore, you must take care of your spirit.

I do not know where you are in your spiritual journey. No matter where you are, I strongly encourage you to read this chapter reflectively and make sure that you put things right with God. You are being offered an opportunity to have God come and live in you. This should excite you more than having the perfect body.

When Our Lord Jesus Christ says something, it is important that we take it seriously. Here is one of the most famous Bible verses that puts everything in perspective:

> "For what profit is it to a man if he gains the whole world, and loses his own soul? Or what will a man give in exchange for his soul?" Matthew 16:26 (NKJV)

Here, Jesus Christ is asking a profound question that everybody must answer. You cannot afford to keep going through life without answering these questions because how your life ends will determine the answer to these questions. Interestingly, the body is not mentioned in this verse. But the soul is what is front and center because the body will finally die and decay, but the soul is going to live forever.

There is nothing more important than your soul, and you should take this seriously. While there is nothing wrong with being successful in this life, if you neglect what is more important, you are going to have all eternity to regret it.

The major assumption that has been throughout this book is that you are a believer in the Lord Jesus Christ. This implies that you have given your life to Him and accepted Him as your Lord and savior. In addition to being born again, you are walking daily with the Lord and bearing the fruit of the Holy Spirit.

Having an eternal perspective is the ultimate goal because, at the end of the day, it is the eternal that matters. People have looked for the fountain of youth over the ages and there is a lot of research right now to understand aging and how to reverse it. Even if we were to find the fountain of youth and drink from it so that we remain young forever, life on earth would still have a lot of changes for us. This is because even reversing aging and making sure that we remain young here on earth, we would still be always going to face many other challenges because we are living in a fallen world with many different problems.

I say all this to emphasize the importance of looking forward to our true and final home, where we will be with our Heavenly Father forever and ever. While life on earth is great, life in heaven is going to be greater and more fulfilling. This is something that all of God's children have to look forward to.

But if you are not yet a child of God, here is your opportunity for you to learn how to become a child of God. Follow instructions that will give you eternal life.

Life does not end when you die. There is an afterlife, and I am going to use this opportunity to tell you about it. Talking about the afterlife is not an indirect way for you to disengage with the present life, but a motivation for you to do make the most of your time on earth. While there are many arguments about which roads lead to God and which God is true, I am not going to dwell on these issues. The reason being that there is not enough room for us to do a comparative study of world religions.

That said, it is essential to note that while popular culture classifies Christianity as a religion and tries to compare it to other religions, the truth is that Christianity is not a religion. Religion is mankind trying to reach out to God; Christianity is the exact opposite, because God is the person who is reaching out to mankind and doing all to redeem us. To enjoy this redemption that God is offering you must follow instructions.

I am writing this with the assumption that you have been reconciled to God and have a relationship with Him. If you do not yet have a relationship with God, I am going to give you the opportunity here to take care of that. This is one of the most important decisions you will ever make and should not be taken lightly. I do not want you to allow the failures of other believers that you might have interacted with to prevent you from getting into a personal relationship with your heavenly father. He has been waiting for you to come home and be reunited with Him.

Here is your opportunity to come home to the fullness of life and abundant life. All that you need and desire is in God, and you will never be forsaken or abandoned.

Let me start by asking you the following question. Do you have a personal relationship with Jesus Christ? This question is being asked because although all roads lead to Rome, not all roads lead to the God of the Bible. Jesus Christ, who is God incarnate, made some exclusive claims when He said:

> "Jesus answered, 'I am the way and the truth and the life. No one comes to the Father except through me.'"
> John 14:6 (NIV)

This is a bold claim, and Jesus Christ died for standing up for this. He is simply saying that if you want a relationship with the God of the Bible, who is also the creator of heaven and earth, you must pass through Him. If you are not yet a follower of Jesus Christ here is your opportunity to do so. I suggest this because it is going to get you connected to the source of all things. You will become spiritually alive and will live forever in the presence of God. Raising your child with the fear of God is the best thing you can do for you and your child.

The first and most important thing to understand is that we have all sinned. In other words, we cannot meet God's perfect standard no matter how hard we try. Have you tried on your own to be good and realized many times how you do not measure up? Do you struggle with a void in your heart that nothing has been able to fill, no matter how hard you have tried? Are you comparing yourself to others and feeling that you are good because you are better than other people? If you answered yes to any of these questions, you need to understand that all of us have sinned, as the following scriptures clearly spell out.

> "For all have sinned and come short of the glory of God." (Romans 3:23)
>
> "For there is not a just man upon earth, that doeth good, and sinneth not." (Ecclesiastes 7:20)
>
> "But we are all as an unclean thing, and all our righteousness as filthy rags, and we all do fade as a leaf; and our iniquities, like the wind, have taken us away." (Isaiah 64:6)
>
> "As it is written, 'There is none righteous, no, not one.'" (Romans 3:10)
>
> "For whosoever shall keep the whole law, and yet offend in one point, he is guilty of all." (James 2:10)
>
> "If we say that we have no sin, we deceive ourselves, and the truth is not in us." (1 John 1:8)

We have all sinned and need God's forgiveness. This is the place to start. When you acknowledge this, then you will be able to receive God's free forgiveness and salvation.

The third crucial thing to understand is the devastating consequences of sin. You may be wondering why sin is such a bad thing and why we are making such a big deal about it. Everybody including you should be concerned about the consequences of sin because according to the following verses sin has a wage, and that wage is death.

> "For the wages of sin is death, but the free gift of God is eternal life in Christ Jesus our Lord." Romans 6:23 ESV
>
> "Therefore, just as sin came into the world through one man, and death through sin, and so death spread to all men because all sinned." Romans 5:12 ESV
>
> "But as for the cowardly, the faithless, the detestable, as for murderers, the sexually immoral, sorcerers, idolaters, and all liars, their portion will be in the lake that burns with fire and sulfur, which is the second death." Revelation 21:8 ESV

This death is both physical and spiritual. Sin can cause us to die in this life, and if we die in sin, we will be separated from God forever. You do not want this to happen to you and your child or children; you want to be able to live forever in the presence of God. This is why the second crucial thing to think about is the wages of sin.

The fourth crucial step is to ask God to forgive your sins. The good news is that God has already made provision to forgive our sins and is ready and willing to forgive us all our sins. As you will soon discover, God has already made the first move.

> "For God so loved the world, that he gave his only begotten Son, that whosoever believeth in him should not perish, but have everlasting life."
> (John 3:16)
>
> "Jesus said unto her, 'I am the resurrection, and the life: he that believeth in me, though he were dead, yet shall he live: And whosoever liveth and believeth in me shall never die. Believest thou this?'"
> (John 11:25-26)
>
> "And they said, 'Believe on the Lord Jesus Christ, and thou shalt be saved, and thy house.'" (Acts 16:31)
>
> "That if thou shalt confess with thy mouth the Lord Jesus, and shalt believe in thine heart that God hath raised him from the dead, thou shalt be saved. For with the heart man believeth unto righteousness, and with the mouth confession is made unto salvation."
> (Romans 10:9-10)
>
> "Whosoever believeth that Jesus is the Christ is born of God: and every one that loveth Him that begat loveth Him also that is begotten of Him."
> (1 John 5:1)

Now that you have confessed and asked Jesus to forgive your sins, your sins have been forgiven and will be remembered no more.

The fifth and final thing to do is invite Jesus into your heart. Now is your opportunity to surrender your life to Jesus and invite Him to come into your heart. Jesus will never force Himself on anyone. He is outside, according to the following scriptures, knocking and waiting for you to invite Him to come in.

> "Behold, I stand at the door, and knock: if any man hear my voice, and open the door, I will come in to him, and will sup with him, and he with Me." (Revelations 3:20)
>
> "But as many as received Him, to them gave He power to become the sons of God, even to them that believe on His name." (John 1:12)
>
> "And because ye are sons, God hath sent forth the Spirit of His Son into your hearts, crying, Abba, Father." (Galatians 4:6)
>
> "That Christ may dwell in your hearts by faith; that ye, being rooted and grounded in love." (Ephesians 3:17)

Jesus Christ is waiting for you to invite Him to come in and you can do that by praying and asking Him to do so. Use your own words to talk to Him or use the following words, called "The Sinner's Prayer" (by John Barnett).

The following prayer expresses the desire to transfer trust to Christ alone for eternal salvation. If its words speak of your own heart's desire, praying them can be the link that will connect you to God.

> "Dear God, I know that I am a sinner, and there is nothing that I can do to save myself. I confess my complete helplessness to forgive my own sin or to work my way to heaven. At this moment, I trust Christ alone as the One who bore my sin when He died on the cross. I believe that He did all that will ever be necessary for me to stand in Your holy presence. I thank you that Christ was raised from the dead as a guarantee of my own resurrection. As best as I can, I now transfer my trust to Him. I am grateful that He has promised to receive me despite my many sins and failures. Father, I take you at your word. I thank you that I can face death now that You are my Savior. Thank You for the assurance that You will walk with me through the deep valley. Thank you for hearing this prayer. In Jesus' Name, Amen."

Praise God, hallelujah! If you just said this prayer, I am super excited for you and want to use this opportunity to welcome you into the kingdom of God and God's family. This is one of the most critical decisions you will ever make because it has eternal consequences. You are now a newborn baby in Christ and need spiritual nourishment to grow in your faith. If you need more information on what to do next, send an email.

Please, you must understand the fundamental nature of this decision you have just made. I want to highlight the fact that the focus has not been for you to join a religion or to become religious. Religion is Man seeking to please God. But here we have presented a picture of God seeking Man. God loved the entire world and gave His son to pay the penalty for our sins. This point is being made so that you understand that you are being called into a personal relationship with Jesus - not just some religious observances. While church membership is essential, it is more important that you establish a healthy and vibrant relationship with Jesus Christ.

Resources for your new walk with God:

Our lives on earth pale in comparison to eternity. There is no comparison at all because eternity has no measure. Even if you live to be more than 100 years old on earth, you will not make it to 200; your life on this side has a limit. Therefore, the best thing to do is to factor eternity into the equation of your life.

This is what you have just done, and I applaud you for that. Now that you have become a child of God, you need to learn how to walk with Him. You need to learn how to love God and know Him.

When we love somebody, we spend time with them, talk to them and get to know them. This is not done in a day, but it takes time. You just started this relationship with your Heavenly Father, and you have to learn how to know Him and grow in intimacy with Him. If you need resources on what to do, here is the best way to contact us: eternalkingdom101@gmail. com

Acknowledgments

I thank my heavenly Father, the God of Abraham, Isaac, and Jacob, for His miraculous intervention during my greatest hour of need. Without Him, I never would have endured the experiences recorded in this book.

My wife and children have been extremely supportive, sacrificing all the many hours it took for me to put my thoughts onto paper; a big thank-you for their love and encouragement. This is not just my story; it is theirs as well. Their constant inquiries as to when the book would be ready motivated me to see it through.

Special thanks to my parents, Abraham and Celine Lekunze, for establishing a strong spiritual foundation for me at an early age. This solid faith grounding made it possible for me to leave my country of birth to come to the United States. My parents "walked the talk" and modeled for me what it means to be a person of character and integrity. I thank them for instilling in me the knowledge of right and wrong and good and evil. Their emphasis on walking the narrow path, accepting delayed gratification, and choosing what is right over what is popular prepared me as I embarked on my journey.

God sometimes uses people to answer prayers, and this book is a product of all the friends who stood by me and my family as we navigated the complexities of America's immigration system. I thank Dr. Anthony Musumba, Dr. Ebenezer Olademeji, Dr. Duane Collins, Dr. Deji Okunlola, Dr. James Carter, Dr. Jonathan Eisenmann, Alice Musumba, Akingbade Akinfenwa, Earl Little, Fabrice and Kandice Mulango, Peju Adedeji, Ruth Collins, Scott Fitzpatrick, Scott Fricks, and Tran Steel.

The staff at Missional University Press did an excellent job of perfecting the manuscript and turning it into a book that is readable; a special thank-you to Terry Wells Bailey for her leadership, encouragement, and prayers.

About the Author

Dr. Eric Tangumonkem was born and raised in a Caldera on the Cameroon Volcanic Line in Cameroon West Africa. He has a Bachelor's degree in Geology and a minor in Sociology from the University of Buea in Cameroon, a Masters in Earth Sciences from the University of Yaounde in Cameroon, and a Doctorate in Geosciences from the University of Texas at Dallas. In addition to being a geoscientist with extensive experience in the oil and gas industry, he is a teacher and an entrepreneur. Currently, he teaches at Embry Riddle, and West Hills College.

He is also the President of IEM Approach, a premier personal growth and leadership development company based on the infinite wisdom revealed over the ages. He is on a mission to inspire, equip, and motivate people from all walks of life to find their God-given purpose, pursue, and possess it. He is married and has five children.

Available for speaking engagements:

If you want to invite Dr. Tangumonkem to speak, you can call him using this number 214-908-3963 or email him at eternalkingdom101@gmail.com

Here are his social media handles:

https://www.erictangumonkem.com

https://www.linkedin.com/in/drtangumonkem/

https://twitter.com/DrTangumonkem

https://www.facebook.com/drtangumonkem

tangumonkem.tumblr.com

https://instagram.com/tangumonkem/

http://www.pinterest.com/erictangumonkem/

https://vimeo.com/user23079930

https://www.youtube.com/c/EricTangumonkem

Eric Tangumonkem, Ph.D.

Other Resources by the Author

Coming to America: A Journey of Faith

Do you struggle with trusting God with your finances? Feel that God is calling you to do something big but you can't see how it will be accomplished? Fear that He has abandoned you after starting your journey of faith? Coming to America: A Journey of Faith is Eric Tangumonkem's story of wrestling with these thoughts and doubts. God called him to America from Cameroon to pursue graduate studies at the University of Texas at Dallas, but he had no money to put towards this dream. In this book, Tangumonkem shares his journey of learning to trust God as he stepped out in faith and came to America despite a lack of funds. He also shares some of his formative experiences prior to this call-experiences that will encourage readers in their faith. Tangumonkem's life is a testimony to the faithfulness of God, and he is careful to give Him all of the glory.

https://www.amazon.com/dp/B082D16PD5/ref=cm_sw_r_tw_dp_x_RXTmFbKTVRZCR via @amazon

The Use and Abuse of Titles in The Church

This book examines reasons behind the disturbing proliferation of titles in Christendom in recent times by seven distinguished Christian professionals. The book challenges readers to stay on the straight and narrow road, which celebrates ministers with titles bestowed based on sound Biblical foundations, while shunning those with titles associated with self-promotion and doctrinal errors. The book also provides the following actionable insights:· How to identify the proper use of titles · A history on the use of titles in Christendom How to avoid the pitfalls of acquiring bogus titles An understanding of the relationship between titles and leadership

https://www.amazon.com/dp/B01E5H36CC/ref=cm_sw_r_tw_dp_x_b4TmFb2K22RPE via @amazon

Seven Success Keys Learned From My Father

This is a book about my father, my teacher, my role model and hero. A man of passion like any other man, but a man of exceptional qualities and abilities as well. The following are the seven keys to success my father passed to me: Fear of God, Humility, Education, Integrity, Hard work, Prayer and Vision. All these keys have been instrumental in making me who I am today. In addition to these keys, my father was present when we were growing up. He made it a point of duty to talk the talk and walk the walk before us. This book illustrates how these seven keys to success were interwoven in our day-to-day lives and how they have opened unprecedented doors of success to me. My sincere prayer for you as you read this book is that these keys will open all doors for you and bring the success you desire so strongly. Amen!

https://www.amazon.com/dp/B01N0A0YYC/ref=cm_sw_r_tw_dp_x_I6TmFbP3QSX91 via @amazon

Viajando a América: Un Camino de Fe (Spanish Edition)

¿Lucha con confiar en Dios con sus finanzas? Siente que Dios le está llamando a hacer algo grande, pero usted no puede ver la forma en que se llevará a cabo? ¿Teme a que Él le ha abandonado después de comenzar su camino de fe?

Viajando a América: Un Camino de Fe es la historia de Eric Tangumonkem, de su lucha con estos pensamientos y dudas. Dios lo llamó a América desde Camerún para realizar estudios de posgrado en la Universidad de Texas en Dallas, pero no tenía dinero para seguir este llamado. En este libro, Tangumonkem comparte su viaje de aprender a confiar en Dios cuando caminó en la fe y llegó a Estados Unidos a pesar de su falta de fondos. También comparte algunas de sus experiencias formativas previas a esta convocatoria-experiencias que estimularán a los lectores en su fe. La vida de Tangumonkem es un testimonio de la fidelidad de Dios, y él tiene cuidado en darle toda la.

https://www.amazon.com/dp/B018H9S2BY/ref=cm_sw_r_tw_dp_x_hdUmFb8QN2148 via @amazon

MON ODYSSÉS AMÉRICAINE: UNE EXPÉRIENCE DE FOI (French Edition)

As-tu du mal à confier tes soucis financiers au Seigneur? Ressens-tu que Dieu t'appelle à faire quelque chose de grand, mais tu ne sais comment cela va se réaliser? Crains-tu qu'il va t'abandonner en chemin? Mon Odyssée Américaine: une expérience de foi est l'histoire d'Éric Tangumonkem et de sa lutte contre le doute et les pensées susmentionnées. Dieu l'a appelé depuis le Cameroun pour aller poursuivre ses études supérieures à l'Université du Texas à Dallas, mais il n'avait pas d'argent pour réaliser ce rêve. Dans ce livre, le Dr Tangumonkem partage avec vous les péripéties de son voyage qui l'ont amené à faire davantage confiance à Dieu alors qu'il se rendit aux États-Unis par la foi. Il partage également certaines des expériences qui l'ont bâti avant même son appel —expériences qui vont encourager les lecteurs dans leur foi. La vie du Dr Tangumonkem est un témoignage de la fidélité de Dieu à qui il rend toute la gloire.

https://www.amazon.com/dp/B00T7XBPMS/ref=cm_sw_r_tw_dp_x_heUmFbZH8NZWN via @amazon

God's Supernatural Agenda: 7 Secrets to Lasting Wealth and Prosperity

Is there something more valuable than money, precious stones, silver, and gold? Do you desire to be wealthy and prosperous? Are you already wealthy and prosperous, yet you feel empty and unsatisfied? Are you uncomfortable talking about money because it is "the root of all evil"? This book will not present shortcuts or get-rich-quick schemes, but important principles, laws, and processes involved in generating lasting wealth.

You see, God desires for ALL of us to prosper today and for all eternity. He has a divine reason for that desire, and He has given us the way to attain it. God's Supernatural Agenda: 7 Secrets to Lasting Wealth and Prosperity presents His blueprint for prosperity and explains why it is what truly matters.

https://www.amazon.com/dp/B07WJLB4BM/ref=cm_sw_r_tw_dp_x_QfUmFb11KQQN0 via @amazon

Racism, Where Is Your Sting?
A provocative look at the beginning and the end of racism

Each time the issue of racism is mentioned, tensions immediately run high, reason is thrown out the window, and emotional outbursts run rampant. Even though a lot of effort has been done to fight it, the devastating consequences continue to this day.

In this book, Dr. Tangumonkem challenges the status quo and presents a perspective that is both provocative and inspirational. Contrary to what you hear from those stoking the flames of racism and fermenting hate and bigotry, we are not at the mercy of racism. In fact, he dives deep into history to explain why the tendency to be racist is present in each one of us, regardless of skin color. The good news is that the victory has already been won — all we need is to live it out. When we stare right at this supercharged issue with fresh, unfiltered eyes, a seismic shift happens. Perhaps, the light at the end of racism is in sight.

https://www.amazon.com/dp/B082D16PD5/ref=cm_sw_r_tw_dp_x_4gUmFbRFX7EQQ via @amazon

The Intersection of Faith, Migration and God's Mission: A call for the people of God in the West to engage in Mission Dei

"Our missionary brothers, sisters, sons, daughters, husbands, and wives would travel thousands of miles to share the gospel to people in faraway lands. They are willing to sacrifice all to share the love of God with these people. Times are changing. Now, God is bringing people from foreign lands right to our shores. Is this a new mission? What is His reason? Unfortunately, the present political climate and rhetoric are making it extremely difficult, if not impossible, for us to have a level-headed discussion when it comes to this topic of migration. It seems the people of God are divided on what to do as well. We have been tasked to be the light of the world. We cannot hide behind nationalistic tendencies or political correctness. We must stand up and be the light in a time of darkness. We must speak the truth in love in a time of fear. We must advocate for peace in a time of hatred."

https://www.amazon.com/dp/B083P5QCW1/ref=cm_sw_r_tw_dp_x_8IUmFbYSP3NR4 via @amazon

Eric Tangumonkem, Ph.D.

Phones, Electronic Devices, and You: Who Is in Charge?

Do you have a serious fear of missing out (FOMO) when you're not online?•Do you have separation anxiety when you don't have your phone with you?•Do you text while driving? •Are your electronic devices on 24/7?If you or someone you know experience these things, read on. It is true that our phones and electronic devices have become part-and-parcel of our lives. It is connecting us in ways unimaginable. Unfortunately, it is also causing a lot of havoc in our relationships because one cannot have meaningful connections with somebody and be on the phone at the same time. This book was written to help you put your phone and electronic devices in the right place, especially when it comes to your interactions with other people. Your world will not crumble if you go offline at the appropriate times. Whose life and relationships are at stake? Yours. Take charge.

https://www.amazon.com/dp/B083P4YHRR/ref=cm_sw_r_tw_dp_x_VmUmFbT4TYCD5 via @amazon

How to Inspire Your Online student: 7 Steps to Achieving Unparalleled Success in An E-Learning Environment

Online teaching and learning are here to stay. We are living in an exciting time, with the opportunity to educate the world at our fingertips. This book makes a case for the need to bring inspiration in the online learning environment, and it explores how far this can go to raise a new generation of students who will have a local and global impact.

The flexibility, versatility, and dynamic nature of online learning holds the key to arriving at global solutions that have a regional signature. While students from all over the world are connected to world-class professors from around the globe, they will be able to receive customized solutions to meet the needs of their individual communities.

While some countries can afford the rising costs of education, others cannot. Even the countries that can afford to educate their citizens are experiencing ever-increasing expenses; one way to cut those costs without compromising quality is through online delivery.

This book explains why and how this is possible and how you, as an online instructor, can play a vital role.

https://www.amazon.com/dp/B08G5BY56D/ref=cm_sw_r_tw_dp_x_y7.qFbTME9W4Q via @amazon

How to succeed as an online student: 7 Secrets to excelling as an online student

How do you know if you have what it takes to study and succeed online? From what I have observed, there is a large chasm between "knowing" and "doing." If knowing was all that was necessary to be successful, all of us would be hugely successful. Fortunately, this book is designed in such a way that it will move you from knowing to doing. Therefore, you should make up your mind to act on the information presented in this book. Without a concerted effort to apply this information, the secrets will not work. The challenge for you might be making the necessary changes to be successful. I hope that this resource will help you succeed in your online courses.

https://www.amazon.com/dp/B08G5BY56D/ref=cm_sw_r_tw_dp_x_qE9vFbXB0ZKAQ via @amazon

Welcome to America: 52 Proven Strategies That Will Position You to Excel as an Immigrant

You are thousands of miles away from your country of birth and will need to learn new skills to adapt to this new culture. You are one among millions who have landed on the shores of this great country in pursuit of "The American Dream." Your success depends heavily on what you do during your first couple of years here.

When I arrived in the US, there was no book like this to give me a springboard to move at the speed of light. That is why this book was written: to help you succeed in a big way.

You have been presented with an opportunity to reinvent yourself, and this process will be directed and implemented by you and nobody else. You will receive much help along the way if you are courageous enough to ask. Besides support from others, you should learn from the get-go that you are the ultimate driver of your boat. How fast you go and how far you reach is up to you. Unlike where you have come from, here, you are expected to take charge and be responsible for your own outcome.

You have sacrificed a great deal to be in the US, and there is no turning back or room for failure. All you must do is follow the time-tested advice you are about to receive; believe it, speak it, act on it, and you will be unstoppable.

The 52 strategies listed in the book are not just for the immigrants who migrate to the United States of America, but for all who migrate within or out of the country and for those with whom the immigrants will be interacting. This is an attempt to maximize the potential that migration brings and lessen the downside that is associated with it.This book presents a holistic approach to health, wealth, and fitness; the physical and spiritual must be in synergy for real, lasting, and sustainable success.

To Exercise or Not to Exercise: The Connection Between Bodily Exercise and Spirituality

"I was given a job and given a horse to get the job done. I overworked my horse; it died, and now I cannot do my job."

This is a story that has influenced me profoundly and spurred this book.

Your body is the horse. Are you taking good care of it? Now is the best time to look after your health; your productivity depends on it.

What is the one thing that will negatively impact your productivity? No matter how talented you are and how lofty your goals, without good health, nothing else matters. While many take their health for granted and assume, they can afford to neglect it, the fact is that they cannot. The cost of ill health is so high, none of us can afford it.

This book presents a holistic approach to health, wealth, and fitness; the physical and spiritual must be in synergy for real, lasting, and sustainable success.

What's in Your Glass? Pentecostal Christians, and the Hidden Dangers of Sugary Drinks

Was the wine made by Jesus equivalent to soda pop?

Is it a sin to consume sugar-loaded drinks?

How can something sweet be bad for your health?

These and many other questions will be addressed in this book.

Most fervent Pentecostal believers do not touch any alcohol. Instead, they focus on being filled with the Holy Spirit; they take this matter seriously and do not compromise. This belief has led many to consume sugary drinks as an alternative to alcohol. There is an assumption that, since these drinks are non-alcoholic, they are safe to consume. In reality, this practice is potentially more problematic.

What's in Your Glass?: Pentecostal Christians, and the Hidden Dangers of Suga...

https://www.amazon.com/dp/B08LST35P1/ref=cm_sw_r_tw_dp_x_T6aZFbQWJNYXZ via @amazon

What Do You Have?: The Secret Of Experiencing Exponential Growth And Productivity

You are thousands of miles away from your country of birth and will need to learn new skills to adapt to this new culture. You are one among millions who have landed on the shores of this great country in pursuit of "The American Dream."

Your success depends heavily on what you do during your first couple of years here. When I arrived in the US, there was no book like this to give me a springboard to move at the speed of light. That is why this book was written: to help you succeed in a big way. You have been presented with an opportunity to reinvent yourself, and this process will be directed and implemented by you and nobody else. You will receive much help along the way if you are courageous enough to ask. Besides support from others, you should learn from the get-go that you are the ultimate driver of your boat. How fast you go and how far you reach is up to you. Unlike where you have come from, here, you are expected to take charge and be responsible for your own outcome. You have sacrificed a great deal to be in the US, and there is no turning back or room for failure. All you must do is follow the time-tested advice you are about to receive; believe it, speak it, act on it, and you will be unstoppable. The 52 strategies listed in the book are not just for the immigrants who migrate to the United States of America, but for all who migrate within or out of the country and for those with whom the immigrants will be interacting. This is an attempt to maximize the potential that migration brings and lessen the downside that is associated with it.

What Do You Have?: The Secret Of Experiencing Exponential Growth And Producti...

https://www.amazon.com/dp/B08MQLRP97/ref=cm_sw_r_tw_dp_x_TcbZFb11B90H6 via @amazon

To order additional copies of this book call:
214-908-3963
Or visit our website at
www.iempublishing.com

If you enjoyed this quality custom-published book
Drop by our website for more books and information

"Inspiring, equipping and motivating one author at a time."

Follow Us

www.ingramcontent.com/pod-product-compliance
Lightning Source LLC
Chambersburg PA
CBHW061331040426
42444CB00011B/2861